M000164581

Worthy To Be Found

An Unforgettable Story of Reunion, Resilience, and Restoration

Worthy To Be Found

An Unforgettable Story of Reunion, Resilience, and Restoration

Deanna Doss Shrodes

Entourage Publishing 2014

Entourage Publishing
www.Entourage-Publishing.com
Redondo Beach, CA 90278

Worthy To Be Found,
An Unforgettable Story of Reunion, Resilience, and
Restoration
By Deanna Doss Shrodes

Copyright 2014 Deanna Doss Shrodes.
All rights reserved.

License Notes
This book is licensed for your personal enjoyment only.
This book may not be re-sold or given away to other
people. If you would like to share it with another person,
please purchase an additional copy for each recipient. If
you're reading this book and did not purchase it, or it was
not purchased for your use only, then please return to
Amazon.com and purchase your own copy. Thank you
for respecting the hard work of the author.

Entourage Publishing, 2014
E-book eISBN: 978-0-9856168-7-8
Paperback ISBN: 978-0-9856168-6-1

Editor: Laura Dennis
www.Laura-Dennis.com

Cover Art by Linda Boulanger (2014)
TellTaleBookCovers.weebly.com

What People are Saying About Worthy To Be Found ...

Worthy to Be Found is sure to become a classic in adoption literature. Author Deanna Doss Shrodes provides an invaluable map for adoptees who are searching, who have ridden the wild ride that reunion can bring, and who are Christians who have been told that post-adoption pain should be spiritualized. How I wish I could have had Deanna's book twenty-years ago.
—Sherrie Eldridge, author

* * *

Worthy To Be Found, An Unforgettable Story of Reunion, Resilience and Restoration, is one adoptee's deeply personal account of the legacy of trauma resulting from the misbegotten, shame-based closed adoption system that existed in the U.S. during much of the twentieth century.

Deanna Doss Shrodes tells us her life story through the lens of being an adoptee who was raised knowing nothing of her true, biological origins. As an adult she seeks to find her birth mother. The resulting journey spans many years and brings her both incredible joy and agonizing pain. Ultimately it is her faith, and the abiding love of her husband, family, community and a Christian therapist, that allows her to heal.

Like many others, I have been privileged to "meet" Deanna through her Adoptee Restoration blog, and have followed the recent events in her adoption story as she lived them and shared them online. So I was completely surprised by how powerfully I was affected by this book. I found myself swept along by her words and holding my breath, even though in many instances I knew what was coming. I felt her passion, her pain, and her abiding commitment to the value of truth and reality.

There is a luminescence of "Deanna-ness" in her writing that makes her words shine. Perhaps it is her faith in God. Or perhaps it is because her writing is just that good.

Deanna is bringing forth what is within her. If you are on a journey to bring forth what is within you, particularly if you are an adoptee or a first/birth mother, this book will be an inspiration and support to you.

—Karen Caffrey, LPC, JD, adoption counseling specialist and writer

* * *

Adult adoptees are the wisest teachers for young adoptees and adoptive parents. Deanna's book, full of wit and wisdom will leave you both laughing and crying, but most of all understanding her journey, which is hers alone, while also being very reflective of so many other adoptees' stories.

—Jane Ballback, mother of three beautiful children from Korea, and Publisher and Executive Editor of *Adoption Voices Magazine*.

* * *

A poignant story of an adopted woman's spiritual and emotional journey of self-discovery. Deanna's book is important addition to anyone's adoption library.

—**Joe Soll, psychotherapist and author of** *Adoption Healing... a path to recovery*

* * *

In *Worthy To Be Found*, Deanna Doss Shrodes shares a message of grace that is affordable to all women "touched by adoption" (and maybe men, too), no matter their religious devotion, and even if they profess non-belief entirely.

The memoir discloses the bare facts of her personal history as an adoptee relinquished toward the end the Baby Scoop Era. Shrodes reveals the full range of her emotional experience during the search and complicated reunion with her birth mother.

What is both significant and unique about this "Christian memoir" is Pastor Shrodes' courageous confrontation of the ages old patriarchal Christian orthodoxy that affords only recriminations and punishment to the girl or woman who is pregnant and unwed. Shrodes' interpretation of scripture tells us that mother and child should be helped as a unit, not separated from each other as a twisted reparation. She counsels that Christ's redemption was meant even for such women and especially for their children. It's a kinder, gentler, perhaps truer Christianity.

—**Corie Skolnick, M.S. LMFT, retired family and marriage therapist, and author of** *ORFAN*, **in development as a major motion picture**

Deanna Doss Shrodes' memoir *Worthy To Be Found, An Unforgettable Story of Reunion, Resilience, and Restoration* is the compelling telling of the author's multifaceted life. Shrodes shares her story with candid grace. She writes with humor and warmth as she takes us from her past to her present. Her story grabs the reader by the heart, races them up her emotional mountain highs, and down into her dark emotional valleys. Shrodes weaves her Christian faith throughout her memoir but much more is revealed in the soul of the book— the ever shifting meaning of family, the crucial need for transparency in an adoptee's life, and the powerful role of community. Although Shrodes' memoir is thematically complex, this book is a quick, easy, and memorable read.

—Diane René Christian, Author of *An-Ya and Her Diary* and Co-founder of The AN-YA Project

* * *

Worthy To Be Found is Deanna's story. Deanna has the gifts of insight, courage, and storytelling, and in Worthy To Be Found, they combine to form a testimony that can bring insight, hope, and healing to its readers. Deanna incorporates her mature faith (Christians are not exempt from pain, healing doesn't always come immediately, and God doesn't waste our stories) with clinically sound insights. (Pain demands to be felt and dealt with, family secrets are very destructive, and we all desperately need friends who are OK with us admitting we're not OK.) Deanna draws from her faith and experience to add third and fourth options to the question of "Nature or Nurture" – we can make our own choices, and God can also intervene.

Worthy To Be Found belongs alongside Lori Holden's *The Open Hearted Way to Open Adoption* and Bryan and Angela Tucker's documentary *Closure* as profoundly insightful and helpful narratives for adoptees, first parents, adoptive parents, and people considering becoming foster or adoptive parents.

—Addison Cooper, LCSW, foster care-adoption supervisor and founder of the blog, *Adoption at the Movies*

* * *

Why would adoptive moms like me want to know the inner thoughts of an adoptee like Deanna Doss Shrodes? *Because such a privileged peek gives us possible insights into the children we are raising.* How helpful is it to glean what could be our children's innermost thoughts about their adoption, their birth parents, their fears and their longings? In entertaining form, Shrodes shares with us what adoption is like *from the inside*. A must-read for anyone with an interest in adoption, faith, or restoration after significant loss.

—Lori Holden, adoptive parent and author *of The Open-Hearted Way to Open Adoption: Helping Your Child Grow Up Whole*

* * *

More than a memoir, more than a human interest story, Deanna Doss Shrodes' *Worthy to be Found* envelopes the reader with gripping and brutally raw honesty. Told painfully like it is, through her truth, the author revels one of the most healthy and reality-based ways to come to terms with the often painful issues faced by those adopted and subsequently searching for their birth families. Without any sugar coating, and augmented with much needed adoption facts, her journey deep into both the pain and the healing can serve as a guide for those on similar trajectories. As a birthmother myself, it is the message that Deanna makes most clear to other mothers that I find to have the greatest value. Her compassion for her own lost mother, her understanding, and forgiveness even for the greatest wounds is a much needed prayer that many need to hear for their own paths to healing. For indeed, in adoption, adoptees have a right to their own truth and the mothers need to know that they are worthy to be found. A must read for anyone who wishes a view into the reality of the adopted.

—Claudia Corrigan D'Arcy, birthmother blogger, and adoptee rights activist at *Musings of the Lame: Exposing Adoption Truths*

* * *

Deanna Shrodes tells her story with gutsy candor and self-depreciating humor. As a result, what should be a bleak and heartbreaking tale becomes a romp filled with resiliency and hope. Deanna's authenticity allows us the courage to examine the trauma of adoption and gain much needed insight into how practices must change. I am grateful for her voice, for she speaks for multitudes of others who have not yet found the courage to share.

—Bonnie Zello Martin, Med, CACS, LCPC, therapist

* * * * * *

For Larry, Dustin, Jordan, and Savanna Rose

*I am so thankful for our family and our secret-free home.
I love you.*

Contents

Worthy To Be Found

An Unforgettable Story of Reunion, Resilience, and Restoration

Preface

"You own everything that happened to you. Tell your stories. If people wanted you to write warmly about them, they should've behaved better."

— Anne Lamott

I own this story.

It happened to me.

Others are a part of it, but this is the story the way I experienced it, with my voice.

I'm sure the others would tell it differently. That is their prerogative.

We all share through the unique lens of our experience.

But this is my story, and no one can change that.

I lived it, and am still living it.

Some people have asked why I chose to write my story, in the first place. There are many reasons, but seven of the most important are:

For the purpose of living transparently. I'm determined to live without secrets. A Christian counselor once told me that family secrets are one of the most destructive things, ever. I have come to believe that and have chosen as far as it depends on me to live without them.

For the purpose of context. When a writer shares her narrative, it provides the framework for everything else that she writes.

For the purpose of helping people who are going through or have gone through anything like this before. Due to what flooded my inbox when this story first published on my blog, Adoptee Restoration, I know there are many people out there who have faced my struggle. I am absolutely blown away and humbled by how many people read this story at the blog. And I'm even more surprised at how many commented or contacted me privately. To all of you who were among that number, I say thank you from the bottom of my heart. Reaching out to let me know you cared was more important than you will ever know. It's because of the cry of the hearts of my blog readers, and a subsequent invitation from Entourage Publishing, that you are reading this book right now.

For the purpose of sharing what I've learned. It's a challenge to do that if people don't know how I ended up here in the first place.

For the purpose of better time management. Upon the launch of Adoptee Restoration, my inbox quickly filled up with e-mail from all over the world. People would ask many questions about my background. It became overwhelming to try to write out the details, which was one factor leading to my decision to write the story.

For the purpose of catharsis. Writing it helped me to process it. Some said, "Couldn't you do that privately?" Yes, but I'm transparent by nature, daring to write what some are afraid to write, and what a lot of people need. I also knew if others were reading along as I wrote, I'd be faithful to continue and write it even when some aspects were hard for me to go to. I needed to face the challenging parts, painful as they were. And I came to realize that it was the revelation of the hardest ones that helped me the most, and ultimately helped other people in the same way too.

For the purposes of God. That's the crux of it, more than anything else. I believe God never wastes anything. He will use my story and yours, for His glory.

Warning!!!

There are times you may become angry while reading my story. You may be tempted in the midst of it to pass judgment. I guarantee it! You may even to be tempted to shut this book, write to me and tell me you think I am a terrible person, or that someone else in my story is such.

Consider reading the story entirely, with all the twists and turns before you write me hate mail.

With that said, let's get started.

Chapter 1—
The Beginning and
the Breakdown

"From all of our beginnings, we keep reliving the Garden story."

— *Ann Voskamp*, One Thousand Gifts: A Dare to Live Fully Right Where You Are

February 28, 2013 was a terrible day.

I've had some pretty tough days and survived. The good news about it is, when you've faced the worst thing ever, it has a way of making you fearless because you know you actually stared it down and survived.

February 28 was a day I ended up going to bed and staying there for three days.

I cried every moment I was awake for three days.

Then I wept for five hours on the fourth day, and three hours on the fifth day.

I was moments away from asking my husband, Larry, to take me to Florida Hospital and check me in.

Thankfully, on the sixth day, I found Melissa Richards. Thanks to God and the help of Melissa as His hand extended, you're reading this right now.

My faith wasn't shaken through this experience—but my life was.

I believe there are times that all of us will be shaken in life. Even our very world is shaken at times, however our faith doesn't have to be. Thankfully, my faith stayed strong through the crisis, though it doesn't mean I didn't feel pain.

Pain demands to be felt, and dealt with.

I wish I could give a *Cliff Notes* version of February 28, 2013, but to share it in context; we have to go there by way of 1965.

In Hindsight

If I could go back as my adult self and be in charge of making the decision for my baby self about which of my families I would end up with—birth or adoptive, I don't know what I'd do. Both family units I come from are dysfunctional. I am who and what I am today by the grace of God. Many people say, "Deanna, you're a miracle!" And you know what? They're right.

The only healthy home I have ever known is the one I live in now. It's the home I've made with my husband and children that we have raised. I was determined when I grew up; I'd do it the way I always dreamed.

Where I Came From

I am adopted. But, that is not the beginning of my life or my story. Every adopted person has a story before their adoptive parents came along. And that story will forever be an important part of them.

My natural mother became pregnant in 1965 and suddenly became homeless. Although she was living with her family, she quickly lost everything because she was pregnant. Ostracized. Shamed. An outcast of society. Banished to live in the Florence Crittenton Maternity home until after I was born.

This maternity home was not located in her town. Prior to her pregnancy she had been living with her family in Richmond, Virginia. After being kicked out, she went to the home in Norfolk, Virginia, several hours away.

My mother went through what she describes as "nine months of living hell" before I was born.

After delivering me and returning home to live and try her best to fit back into society, she told me she was kicked out yet again a few months later. What did she do to cause this? Nothing, according to her. Her father apparently just couldn't handle the fact that she had given birth to me. The shame that my birth had taken place was too much for the family to bear, although she had moved several hours away to live while pregnant, and had delivered me in secret. So out she went.

Unmarried. Jobless. Homeless. Nowhere to go.

The Reality for MILLIONS

What my mother faced was not unusual for the 1960s.

From approximately 1940 to 1970, it is estimated that up to four million mothers in the United States surrendered newborn babies to adoption—two million during the 1960s alone. These astronomical adoption numbers are the reason this era is referred to by many as the "Baby Scoop Era." To give a comparison of present day numbers, the National Council for Adoption estimates that 20,000 infants are placed for adoption in the US every year.

The treatment my mother endured was not unique. During this period of time, it was unthinkable for a young lady to let anyone know of her situation. The pregnancy was hidden at all costs. These young ladies were not simply "encouraged" by parents, relatives, pastors, and other authority figures that they needed to "consider" adoption. They were told it was the only option. Keeping their babies and raising them was out of the question.

Some woke up from general anesthesia during labor to find their babies gone—taken without them even being able to ever see them!

Millions of girls and women were told that because they had sinned, they must "do the right thing" as a consequence, surrendering their baby as a "gift" to a childless married couple. In doing so they would have a new start and God would "redeem their mistake." Some pregnant young ladies are still given this treatment today, though it is not as widespread as it was in years gone by.

My Adoption

I was in foster care for two months after my birth, and went on to be adopted through the Children's Home Society of Virginia in a closed, domestic adoption.

I would describe the home I was raised in as a very conservative, Pentecostal home.

If you were a girl or woman, wearing pants in church was out of the question. (And sometimes, wearing pants— period.) Piercing your ears or wearing makeup was a no-no as well. Going to the movies was out. If you dared to be in a movie theatre, you better pray you weren't there during the second coming. ~~Because Jesus wouldn't be able to find you there. Poor Jesus. He's got the whole world in His hands, yet He can't find His way around a movie theater.~~

I was told that my adoptive mother was the first in our home church to wear open-toe shoes, which was a scandal back in the day.

When I was a little girl I was kind of eccentric, often wearing attire such as culottes—an acceptable alternative to shorts—a combination of a skirt and shorts. Pentecostal girls of yesteryear are all too familiar with these. (Needless to say I wouldn't be caught dead in a pair of culottes today.) Usually I had two ponytails on either side of my head, and was always self-conscious that my nose was way too big for my face. When our gym classes at school had any kind of dancing, we opted out for religious reasons. This type of worldly activity was simply unacceptable.

I know my parents meant well with all of this, as it was just what they knew and how they had been taught was the "acceptable way to serve God."

In my senior high school years I was allowed to wear make-up although I remember my mom crying profusely when my dad finally let me get my ears pierced. This was a sure-fire sign that the devil had his hold on me. At the Wednesday night service after I got my ears pierced, Mom tearfully requested prayer for me. (It's rather funny, many years later Mom got her own ears pierced and started wearing makeup.)

And yet amongst all that legalism...

I Found Jesus

I saw. I heard. I experienced.

I felt God's presence and power.

I witnessed the change He could make in someone's life, if only they would make that choice.

As a small child, I often fell asleep under a church pew during nightly revival meetings, covered by one of the altar cloths as service went on late into the night. Sometimes I'd wake up and see a miracle in someone's life taking place right in front of my eyes. (My family was fond of sitting on the first or second row.) I saw physical healings take place. Suffice it to say these are the things one doesn't forget.

I had a relationship with Jesus—a real one, from the time I was a child. Most of what I know about God and the Bible I didn't learn in Bible College, although I appreciated my time there. I learned the majority of what I know in Sunday School, Children's Church, a program called "Missionettes," Youth Group, kids and youth camps, and through the example of faithful Christians who served the church and loved me.

We were extremely faithful church attenders, even on vacation. Our family was present every time the doors were open and even when they weren't! We were always serving, stepping up to help the church in whatever way we could. Staying home from church was rare to non-existent in our lives. Even when we were sick, that was what the altar was for! We believed in divine healing and in the miracle working power of God. Praying for and receiving such was a regular occurrence.

I am particularly thankful for the steadfast example of my adoptive maternal grandmother. She lived across the street and during my younger years had a major hand in raising me. She taught me the most about Jesus—real

Jesus, not fake-rules-based Jesus. She is the Godliest woman I have ever met and although she has passed on, she remains my greatest mentor.

The Break-Up

Although my adoptive parents were (and still are) both church leaders, our home ended up completely crumbling in dysfunction and divorce.

Family secrets caused the disintegration of my adoptive home as well. I often refer to my parents' generation as "The Generation of Secrets." I can only speak to how this affected me personally and that is to say that when one or both of your parents are unhealed and do not get proper help, it affects everyone and everything in the home.

It was one of the worst moments of my life when my mother and I came home from a Wednesday evening service at church and found a note on the dining room table. It simply said, "I'm gone," and bore my father's signature. He left that night, moved 837 miles away and started over.

Our family had problems, but at least prior to the divorce, I had a place to call home. When my mother told me my father had filed for divorce after leaving, I still remember sitting in our family room, when she said, "Are you okay?" and I just choked out through sobs, "No. I always thought I'd have a place to call home and now I don't." That was all I could say and she had nothing she could say to console me.

There was nothing left to say. It was over. They got divorced and sold the house.

For one who is adopted, any loss is greatly magnified.

Viewing my adoptive parents' divorce as an informed, forty-something woman versus an in-the-dark teenager, I see things differently now. Understanding my father's decision after having facts I was not privy to as a child doesn't mean an absence of heartache. Nobody desires a broken home, even for what may be a justifiable or even a biblical cause.

With that said—although it may have been necessary, my father is sorry for how the divorce hurt my sister and me. He feels sorrow for the compounded significant losses in our lives, and wishes things could have been different for us. I have learned through experiences with both my natural and adoptive families just how accurate the Christian counselor's words were about the destructive nature of family secrets. This is the main reason I refuse to have secrets in the home I share with my husband and children.

An All-Too-Common Story

Sadly, many adoptive homes experience dysfunction and divorce. Unfortunately, it's not a rarity—even in Christian homes.

When couples who are adoptive parents get divorced, my heart goes out first to their children because I realize the compounded loss for the adoptee.

Each time I go back to Baltimore I drive by and sit and stare at the house I grew up in. It wasn't a perfect home by far, but at least it was familiar... what I knew. At the moment of my adoptive parent's divorce, I never thought I'd face any worse pain but some things unfortunately trumped this heartache.

Things like February 28, 2013...

Chapter 2—
Growing-Up Adopted

"Those who do not have power over the story that dominates their lives, the power to retell it, rethink it, deconstruct it, joke about it, and change it as times change, truly are powerless, because they cannot think new thoughts."

— Salman Rushdie

I don't speak for all adoptees.

Our stories are not identical.

I am the expert on my personal story, but I'm not one on other people's stories or their adoption.

Every adoptee is different, and the institution of adoption complex. Even so, it's amazing the commonalities found in the community. Thousands of adoptees I've personally connected with share similarities too numerous to list.

I always knew I was adopted. One of the things my adoptive parents did right was to tell me from the very beginning, when I was so young I can't even remember the first time.

Although I always knew I was adopted, I didn't always know that I had another name. When hiding under my parent's bed during a childhood game I felt something cold and heavy. Pulling it out into the light, I discovered a black fireproof box. Upon opening it I found my adoption papers and my legal name change papers. It was then that I realized that the first name I ever had was not Deanna Lynn Doss.

My original name was Melanie Lynn Alley.

I asked my adoptive parents about it and they told me that when they adopted me, they changed my legal name as well. As is customary in a closed adoption, my original birth certificate, bearing the correct information about my birth was altered and sealed.

My adoptive family consisted of my father and mother and my younger sister who was also adopted, four years later. We were both adopted from the Children's Home Society of Virginia. (We did not come from the same original mother and father.) My adoptive family has a large extended family on both sides, my mother's family from Baltimore, Maryland and my father's hailing from Tuscaloosa, Alabama. I spent many weeks in the summertime visiting relatives in the tiny little town within Tuscaloosa where my father grew up and moved back to after the divorce—Berry, Alabama.

After adopting my sister and me, our parents moved from Virginia to Baltimore, Maryland, settling our family in my adoptive mother's hometown, near a large portion of her family. Most of the family were not only members, but very active in ministry in some way at our home church, Bethel Assembly of God.

My adoptive great grandfather was partly responsible for both the start of our church, and for building the house where I grew up.

I was raised in Baltimore County on the Chesapeake Bay in an area called Jones Creek, home to lots of blue crabs (steamed, yum! yum!) and Bethlehem Steel. Our house was located at 7316 North Dakota Avenue, and my grandmother, Jura Lewis, and her family was actually responsible for naming our street as they had originally hailed from North Dakota. Just one street over from North Dakota was Bayfront Road, reason being, the Chesapeake Bay was right there.

As a kid I would leave my bedroom window open a little bit on most nights and could hear the sounds across the water, mostly from Bethlehem Steel, as I would drift off to sleep. While Baltimore is a huge city, Jones Creek was the kind of place where everybody knew everybody.

Everyone in Jones Creek knew Jura Lewis, otherwise known as "Sister Lewis" or "Grandma Lewis." She cut your kids' hair, cared for your children, taught your Sunday School class, helped you when you were sick, baked a pie for you, and most certainly she had prayed for you at some time whether you knew it or not.

Another Face like Mine

My features were very different from everyone in my adoptive family.

I constantly searched for a familiar face that I had never seen before.

I realize to non-adoptees that sounds like an oxymoron but adoptees will understand.

Throughout my life, people have asked, "Are you Italian?" upon first meeting me. For most of my life, I had no idea of my ancestry and would just answer that I didn't know, being that I am adopted. (It was later confirmed through several means, that although I do have Italian blood, my paternal family is predominantly Greek. This explains my distinct features and why so many asked me that question.)

As a kid we would occasionally go to baseball games in Baltimore City (it was Memorial Stadium back then). While everyone around me watched the game, I would gaze into the sea of thousands of faces that surrounded me. When someone passed by who possessed certain physical traits, I would wonder if they were my natural mother or father.

It was illogical that my natural family members would be there. They didn't live near Baltimore. But you wonder about a lot of illogical things when you are adopted.

Because you just don't know.

And when you don't know, your mind wanders to all sorts of options, grasping for anything to hold onto.

There is a term for this. It's called genetic mirroring. Author Rebecca Hawkes explains it as she shares, "Genetic mirroring is one of the ways that human beings make sense of who we are and define our identities, by observing people who share our genetic make-up."

I have heard it said that every adoptee searches. Some openly search and others search only in their minds, but all of them search.

Whether in my hometown or vacationing far away, I studied faces a lot. Always wondering if they might happen to be there.

Of course I never approached anyone, although sometimes I wanted to. I stayed quiet about this. Always quiet.

As an adoptee, you learn to smile and nod when ladies just trying to make conversation come up and ooohh and ahhhhh saying, "She looks just like you!" to your adoptive mother or sister, who look absolutely nothing like you. Your mother's face lights up because there's nothing in the world she's ever wanted to hear more.

Meanwhile, you are thinking, "It's not true, it's really not true. They are just being nice."

But you don't say that.

Because you believe it would kill your mother emotionally and that is the biggest no-no of all as an adoptee. It is in your psyche that you MUST be a "good adoptee." That means a quiet one who says nothing of these sorts of things. You sense that to be brave enough to say, "I am curious to see a face that looks like mine," is a betrayal of sorts. Adoptees don't get a memo or anything about it, we just know—it's an unwritten rule.

I was a unique little girl who did things like rewrite *I Dream of Jeannie* scripts after school. Who lay on the floor in front of the bookcase reading encyclopedias and Shakespeare. Always creating. Always writing.

Expressions of the soul uniquely manifested themselves from the very beginning, mainly through my art in its various forms. Singing, playing the piano, songwriting, writing creative essays—these were all talents that came bursting forth, announcing themselves before I even had any formal training.

My adoptive parents had records they would play on the stereo—33's of Southern gospel greats such as the Happy Goodmans. They would play those records and my hands would go up and down the piano, finding their way to exactly where they needed to be, to the delight of those watching and listening. I remember when I was a preschooler, singing, "I Wouldn't Take Nothin' For My Journey Now," by Vestal Goodman. It was one of the first songs I sang. The beginning lyrics of the first verse are:

> *I started out traveling for the Lord many years ago.*
>
> *I had a lot of heartaches, had a lot of troubles and woe...*

If I recall, I was four-years-old when I first sang the song. I used to laugh when I thought that I was just a small child singing lyrics about such personal upheaval. But recently a friend said, "Think about it, Deanna... that was actually a perfect song for you at the time!" Already at just a few years old, I had experienced what is referred to in the adoption world as "the primal wound"—the abrupt separation from my first mother, and loss of my entire first family, my name and more.

People would shake their heads in amazement as I played the piano, asking, "How do you find those chords? Where did you learn to play those runs up and down the keys?"

Sometimes other piano players—adults— would say, "Show me how to do that..."

And I'd say, "I don't know how to, and I can't really explain it. I just know where to go. For some reason, my hands find their way and I don't even have to think about it."

From the time I was young, people would gather around the piano for sing-a-longs. If I heard a song even once I could play it, and for that matter I didn't even have to hear it once. I could find exactly where people were in a song if they began to sing it, and follow them, intrinsically knowing where they were headed without ever hearing the song before.

My elementary school music teacher, Mrs. Sue Wilson, quickly discovered my talent and put me to work playing spontaneous "fillers" as she called them before and after shows at Chesapeake Terrace Elementary, and as students were walking on and off of risers. I can still see Mrs. Wilson's huge smile and hear her say, "I'm so proud of you!"

Teachers are responsible for shaping my life in a huge way. I credit my high school choral teacher, Mrs.

Homeretta Ayala, for bringing me from the place of being an awkward and sometimes bullied middle schooler to someone who was accepted by my peers in high school. In seventh and eighth grade I was pushed down flights of stairs by a small but influential and popular group of girls. The original Regina George and her crew from *Mean Girls*. I was often teased about my nose that was too large for my face or the fact that my clothes weren't always in style. They didn't have rules about bullying back then like they do now. I told another favorite teacher, Mrs. Anderson, what was happening and she explained she wanted so very much to help me, but she had to actually catch them in the act in order to do something about it. It was just different back then. Bullies were careful to do things where teachers couldn't see, in places like stairways.

I was pathetically uncoordinated at sports and always picked last for any team.

Couldn't hit a ball to save my life.

Dreaded getting in the showers with all of the girls at the end of gym class.

The same group would heckle for most anything.

The size of your nose.

Your breasts.

It could be anything. They just singled someone out and that was it.

My grandmother cared for me each day before and after school during elementary school. I unabashedly tell people I have absolutely no doubt I am here today because of my grandmother's prayers.

When I was a teenager and old enough to decide whose home to go to after school, I often went to hers instead. It was she who comforted me after being pushed down the stairs one day, when I ran home from school trying to make it in the door before dissolving into tears. A few hours after we talked, she came in and gave me a poem she had written and made pretty with construction paper. It was called "Hope." I still carry one of her writings in my wallet today, though frayed and torn. The poem is called "Let God Use You." It reminds me of what is most important.

"Let God Use You"

There are two mind sets
leading to two kinds of life
and to two ends in life.
Like any fork in the road,
these two courses begin close together
and end far apart.

The one is determined to use God;
The other is willing to be used by God.
"Use God" when it is convenient or safe or useful
and you will miss the Glory
lose the blessing
and live in the shadows.

"Be used by God" when He wills and as He directs,
disturbing your safe routine,
upsetting your small comforts,

denying the less that He may give the more;
then you will see the glory that transforms life,
you will inherit the blessing that outlasts life, and
you will walk in the light as He is in the light.

Don't use God—that's a blind alley.
Let Him use you—that's the road to glory.

The Impact of Teachers

Ms. Julienne Brownrigg was my high school English
teacher for several years and had a huge impact on my
life as well. Anybody who had Ms. Brownrigg for a
teacher will remember her journals. All of her students
had the assignment of a daily journal, written privately to
her. We could talk about whatever we wanted, but we
must write, to her, every day. We did this all year long
and she wrote back to each of us in sidebar comments. I
don't know how in the world she kept up with it. Her
comments back to me literally changed my life. I shared
in the journal many of the feelings I had about life,
school, my family, adoption, hurts and fears, and my
future. Things I could share with no one else. We all
knew that Ms. Brownrigg's journal was a safe place.

Mrs. Homeretta Ayala discovered my vocal talent the
first few weeks of freshman year at Sparrows Point High.
She quickly assigned me a solo for a school-wide
assembly, and it brought the entire student body to a
standing ovation. There was a significant shift after that
day. It was rather amazing. Just moments after singing
the song, a boy asked me out! Just weeks later, I was
elected president of my high school choir by my peers,
when I was only a freshman. I did not struggle with

acceptance the rest of high school. As the Bible says, my gift "made room for me." Part-time jobs doing what I loved opened up for me, such as serving as a substitute organist/pianist at the local Disciples of Christ church, or at Mrs. Ayala's Presbyterian church when she was on vacation. As long as I could play for those services and make it back in time for the service at Bethel, my parents allowed me to accept the invitations. I would go on to play, sing, record professionally and direct choirs in the years to come.

But the expression of all of these talents began almost after I first began to talk.

The answer everyone around me gave was, "Talent comes from God."

I believe all of us are gifted by God. Whether adopted or not, that is so. I also believe nature and nurture play a part. Years later, in reunion, the pieces of the puzzle would be filled in as I learned of all my maternal family members with musical talent.

Issues, Issues, I've Got Issues!

As a child, I had a lot of what are referred to in the adoption or counseling world as "post-adoption issues," but they were never recognized as such until I was an adult and received counseling in order to move forward.

My adoptive mother told me that when they brought me home from the Children's Home Society, I would eat, and eat, and eat. She said I would never stop even if it was definitely clear I had more than enough. I probably would have eaten ten jars of baby food if she let me. I never closed my mouth or pushed away the spoon like most babies do. She portioned out how much food was appropriate for a child (and usually gave a little bit more) and said, "Okay, that's enough," and stopped.

I struggled with emotional eating and binging into adulthood – but never knew why until I received help as an adult.

I bit my nails down to the quick, until they bled, every day. Until I was eighteen. I knew Larry wanted to propose to me, but would rather not put a ring on a bloody finger. My best friend from college, Joanne MacDurmon Greer (who is still a very close friend today), can attest to my struggle with this in preparing to get engaged, and the final breakthrough. I worked so hard with hers and Larry's help to have nice hands (that didn't bleed) for Larry to give me my engagement ring.

To this day if you ask Larry, "What's the physical feature you love most about your wife?"

He will say, "Her hands. I love my wife's hands." He tells me all the time how beautiful they are. He does tell me that other parts of me are beautiful as well, but he is so proud of me for my hands.

I wet the bed almost every night until first or second grade. My grandma was the one who ultimately helped me to stop and get this under control.

Goodbyes were always a horrible trigger. I learned since then that this is not uncommon for adoptees. I was always afraid of goodbyes or being left behind—purposefully or accidentally. This was another post-adoption issue I received help for as an adult—and overcame.

My First Camp Experience and Mrs. Blagg

During all of my growing up years, I attended church camp at Potomac Park Assemblies of God Camp in Falling Waters, West Virginia. My first experience with camp was quite a memorable one. I went on to attend every year and ultimately received a confirmation of my call to ministry there. But if my first time at camp hadn't been handled correctly, perhaps I wouldn't have ever wanted to return. Even if I did return, I might not have received the amazing blessings God had for me, because of my fears.

My first year of camp, I became fearful that my parents weren't going to come back for me, or that they wouldn't be able to find me at the camp when they returned. As a young child, they never gave me a reason to believe they wouldn't return. They were good, faithful parents in this regard. Nevertheless, I remember lying awake late into the night, worried sick about their return. Would they come back to get me on Saturday when camp was over? Would they be able to find me?

I would pack and repack my suitcase before lights out. My nightly self-assigned chore was organizing and reorganizing it to get it "just right." I now see that this was probably an effort to try to have some sense of control.

As the week of camp progressed, I would lie in bed and quietly cry because amidst all the fun and chaos of lots of little girls staying together, my washcloth had gone missing. Suddenly, I had lost a piece of what control I thought I had.

One of the girls in the cabin heard me crying and asked what was wrong. I couldn't explain it but just said I had lost the washcloth, and was afraid I wouldn't have everything in perfect order. I told her that I was afraid my parents weren't coming back, or that they wouldn't be able to find me if they did return. Noticing my distress, she said, "Let's go get Mrs. Blagg."

Mrs. Blagg was our counselor for the week. I attended camp dozens of other times after that, but interestingly, I don't remember even one counselor's name besides Mrs. Blagg. Thankfully it's for a good reason.

Mrs. Blagg was the hands and feet of Jesus. After the girls ran and got her, she came over to my bunk bed and put an arm around me, asking what was wrong. When I told her my fears, she gently pushed my long brown hair out of my eyes, and wiped my tears. In a soft, comforting voice she said, "Deanna, everything is going to be alright. We will find your washcloth and your parents will find you on Saturday. I promise you—they are coming back for you, and I will be right here with you when they return. It's going to be okay." Then she prayed with me and I was able to be at peace and go to sleep.

She didn't tell me I was silly.

Didn't laugh at me.

Didn't dismiss my fears.

Didn't tell me to suck it up.

I stopped worrying about the washcloth and my parents' return.

I trusted what Mrs. Blagg told me and from that moment, I was able to concentrate on receiving what God had for me at camp.

Mrs. Blagg was Jesus to a little girl at camp who was scared out of her mind that her parents were never going to find her again.

I never forgot Mrs. Blagg. And I sure did love camp! I couldn't wait to go back, again and again!

Reconnecting with Mrs. Blagg

As I was writing my story, I suddenly remembered that we have an Assemblies of God minister that Larry and I serve with in Tampa who also has the last name, Blagg. The AG is a small world even though there are millions of adherents. So, I thought to myself, "Wouldn't it be crazy if Pastor Bruce Blagg is related to Mrs. Blagg?" So... I Facebook messaged him and said, "Hey Bruce, by any chance did your mother ever serve as a camp counselor at Potomac Park Camp? And does your mother have red hair?" To my utter shock, he answered, "Yes!"

Pastor Bruce's mother is Mrs. Joan (pronounced Jo-Ann) Blagg, now in her eighties, and is STILL teaching a Girls Ministries class in her local Assemblies of God church in Idamay, West Virginia.

Bruce immediately got on the phone with her and his father, and read them the story I had sent to him on Facebook. All three of them wept tears of joy!

Mrs. Blagg said, "Bruce, there's more… I served for four years at that camp, but only counseled the first year. The remaining years they placed me in different areas of ministry besides camp counselor. My only time serving as counselor with the girls was the first year—the year with Deanna. It seems God may have had me there just for her sake!"

Bruce asked if I could call him and said he had something special to tell me. Voice breaking with tears, he relayed this story to me and said, "Deanna, that's how much God loves you! He had Mom there that year, just for you!"

Since that time, Mrs. Blagg and her husband, Buck, came to Tampa to visit Bruce and his wife, Pam, and we had the joy of reconnecting.

Post-Adoption Issues in Adulthood

Although a strong person of faith, I still had some unresolved issues well into adulthood. I struggled with depression, anxiety, fear, workaholism, and perfectionism. One-by-one these had to be properly addressed in order to move forward. With God and the right kind of help, anything is possible!

Anyone who has been in or around ministry for very long knows that transitions in the church—any church, are common. It's my least favorite part of ministry. For years, before I received help—my way of coping with this was to hide or avoid a goodbye at all cost.

None of these things were diagnosed as post-adoption issues when I was growing up, but it's exactly what they were. As an adult, I went to two Christian counselors and even the mention of my adoption being related to any of this was immediately brushed off. Both held the view that adopted children were no different than any other child, required no additional help to thrive, and failed to see the loss related to relinquishment and adoption. Both were licensed Christian therapists operating at a reputable counseling center. I said to the second counselor, "Did you hear me say that I'm adopted, when we began the session?"

He said, "Yes, I did." And then he moved right along as if I had just said that I take two teaspoons of cream in my coffee.

Like many adoptive parents of that era, my parents were under the impression that adopted children needed no special help. This was because they weren't informed about post-adoption issues, by the adoption agency or anyone else. Society did a good job of keeping them uninformed about the fact that their children may have special needs as a result of being relinquished and adopted.

My adoptive mother once told me that the social worker assigned to my case told them, "Bring her home and raise her as any other child. She will need no special treatment."

My parents were in the dark. I don't blame them for what they didn't know.

Solidifying my Faith

I had a strong relationship with Jesus, having accepted Him into my life as a very young child. I did experience some challenges as a teen that led to asking God many questions, searching things out for myself. I learned that God is not afraid of my questions, doubts or fears.

Through it all, I felt His presence. I heard His voice. I found Him for myself and followed Him wholeheartedly. He wasn't just my "family's God," nor was I simply swallowing what I was told without proving it out for myself.

My faith grew. I came to realize what I possessed was a faith that works, in all seasons and circumstances.

Some adoptees, in their loss and pain, have kissed God and the church goodbye, but I didn't end up making that choice. I came to realize the goodness of God personally, and His extravagant love toward me. I am thankful that I have been able to separate the losses I have experienced from God's actions toward me.

I know God is good. I know He loves me. This, I have not doubted. I have doubted people many times, but I know God is good!

The Call of God

I was called into the ministry when I was a child. As I was sitting in my grandmother's backyard one day, at about seven-years-old, I sensed God's call. I wrestled with this over the years at times, but came to a firm decision at sixteen-years-old after several strong confirmations, determining to follow wherever God would lead me.

One confirmation occurred at youth camp and the other in a Sunday night service where Karen Wheaton was ministering, on April 22, 1984. I practically ran from the back row to the altar that was absolutely packed with people at the close of the service. Karen did not know me—had never met me before, but called me out of the crowd. She gave a word that the hand of God was upon my life and He desired to use me in amazing ways for His glory. After that service, she asked to talk to me in the pastor's office for a few minutes and encouraged me about giving everything to follow a call into ministry. She said there was a clear, undeniable call on my life for ministry and exhorted me to leave the influences and relationships behind that had been holding me back. I did so—overnight! I surrendered absolutely everything over to God, and I was never the same. That was one of the most powerful nights of my life, shaping my destiny.

Bible College

Within days after my experience at the service with Karen Wheaton, I started the process of applying to Bible College. Shortly thereafter I was on my way to Valley Forge Christian College (AG) in Phoenixville, Pennsylvania (now known as The University of Valley Forge), where I became a pastoral studies and music major. Not long after arriving, I met Joanne, a student from Philly. We enjoyed everything together from late night girl talks to studying. Joanne and I had decided at the end of freshman year not to date anyone the next year and to seriously focus on our studies and ministry. We had made this choice abundantly clear to everyone and had lived it out for quite a while. But then I started working in the school kitchen…

Meeting Larry

Larry Shrodes, a freshman, worked in the back of the kitchen, washing pots and pans. I worked in the front room washing silverware. Rick Rochkind, an upperclassman, worked with him and they talked as they washed and dried.

"Who is that girl?" Larry asked him one night as I walked by.

"Oh, that's Deanna Doss."

"I want to date her," Larry said.

"Not possible," Rick said. "She and her best friend, Joanne MacDurmon, have this 'thing'—some kind of pact—where they aren't dating anyone, to focus on ministry."

"I *will* date her," Larry confidently said.

With that he started coming around the silverware room, singing silly songs and making jokes. I thought he was hilarious. His sense of humor was enticing but I had no intention of dating him, or anyone.

Soon the time came for me to leave my job in the kitchen. I was struggling to make ends meet working in the kitchen, and had found a job in downtown Phoenixville as a waitress at a place called Mansion House. On my last night of washing silverware, Larry danced his way into the room singing, "Farewell my kitchen love, farewell," to the tune of Michael Jackson's "Farewell My Summer Love." (He has no singing talent so it made it even more comical.)

It came time to leave that night after work and I went to the back room to put my coat on. He walked up and took the winter scarf that was around my neck, placing it around his. It was brand new, only worn once. I had scraped a few dollars together to get a purple plaid scarf that caught my eye at the King of Prussia Mall.

"Hey! Give it back!" I said.

"Go out with me, and I'll give it back!" he said, and walked out.

(I never got the scarf back. It's folded neatly in his top dresser drawer. He considers it a precious heirloom, a reminder of that night—and won't give it up. Larry is actually more sentimental than I am.)

Through a hilarious set of twists and turns that would be a book in itself, I finally broke the "no dating pact" I had made with Joanne and began seeing Larry every hour possible. (In Bible College basically that was every moment we weren't sleeping or working our jobs. Like many bible college couples at the time, we organized our class, meal, and chapel seat assignments so we could be together throughout the day.)

After a year of dating, Larry surprised me in June of 1986 by arranging for a friend to bring me to the beach at sunset in Avalon, New Jersey. When I walked up onto a gazebo, he suddenly appeared wearing a tuxedo and holding a small black box. Opening the box, he asked me to be his wife.

Engaged but Separated

More than anything I wanted the stable, Godly family I had always dreamed of. I was determined nothing was going to stop me from achieving that goal, as well as having just the kind of wedding I wanted. I only planned on doing this once!

Larry's former youth pastor, Randy Visconti and his wife Dawn, had recently accepted the position as directors of New Morning Ministries, an Assemblies of God home for troubled teen girls—former runaways, in Newark, New Jersey. NMM needed a counselor and choir director and I desperately needed a job to pay for our wedding. Wanting to marry Larry sooner rather than later, I made this move and worked at NMM for that year. It was one of the greatest years of my life. Although Larry and I were separated during our engagement, we made that choice in order to be back together sooner as a married couple. We could have just gone to the Justice of the Peace and gotten married, but I didn't want to sacrifice my dream wedding on the altar of having no money and being in a hurry. So, I made this transition—especially since it would enable me to serve in a ministry that I considered a dream opportunity of helping the young ladies and directing the choir.

We married on June 27, 1987 at my home church in Baltimore. Larry and I were just nineteen- and twenty-years-old, respectively. The thought never even occurred to either one of us about how young we both were at the time.

Joanne was my maid of honor. Mrs. Ayala and Mrs. Brownrigg were both there for the occasion. In fact, Mrs. Ayala played the organ. Although we had a special relationship, I felt it was only right that we pay her for all of the work she did for the wedding ceremony. As we stood in the back of the sanctuary just prior to taking pictures, she walked up and placed the envelope with the check back in my hands and said, "Don't insult me! This is an honor!" She threw her arms around me and told me how proud she was of me and how much she loved me.

Larry and I had no money to speak of that summer, in fact neither of us even had jobs when we got back from our honeymoon. Looking back I realize this was incredibly foolish, but at the time it seemed like the most logical thing in the world. Larry started painting buildings at the college to make ends meet and months later, I got a job at National Liberty Corporation as assistant to the director of corporate communications. We lived in what may be classified as the tiniest apartment ever in the married student housing at the college. We possessed no furniture but a rocking chair in the corner and a small glass topped table where we ate. We were soon down to just a rocking chair in the corner, after Larry put a hot pot on the glass tabletop and it shattered.

We didn't even have a bed. (Note: it's a bad idea to get married and not have a bed.) Thankfully, Joanne's dad sold furniture and ended up feeling bad for us after she told him we didn't have a bed. So he gave us a mattress from his store. The mattress on the floor was our bed for the first year. Looking back, those were some of the happiest days of our lives. We were high on love, which took away the sting of reality of having very little, materially.

During this time, we became pregnant with our first child later in the fall and faced our first sorrow together as a married couple when the baby was lost to a miscarriage in December. It took about a year for me to emotionally come to terms with the loss of the baby.

As our first year of marriage was coming to a close, the Viscontis transitioned from New Morning Ministries to become the lead pastors at Calvary Assembly of God in Pennsauken, New Jersey. They invited Larry and me to come on staff as their youth and music pastors. We lived in a parsonage next to the church. During this time Larry and I were both working two jobs to make ends meet, as the church couldn't pay us full-time. In addition to serving in the church, he worked at a place called Rivercrest, and I worked at the U.S. Probation Office in Camden as a clerk. We were busier than ever with four jobs between us, but we were loving life and each other and look back on those times as some of the very best.

In February of 1989 we became pregnant with Dustin, our first born son.

Being pregnant and carrying the baby to term was a huge trigger for me. I didn't even know what a trigger was at that time, but in hindsight it's clear what I was experiencing. Progressing through the stages of pregnancy brought all kinds of emotions to the surface about my adoption.

Dustin is the first blood relative I ever met that I remembered. (I was too young to remember my natural mother the first time we "met" before I was adopted.)

Dustin's eyes were the first I ever looked into and recognized something in them of myself. My son bears the distinction of being the first blood relative that I laid eyes on, with the realization that I was looking into the face of someone who had a genetic link to me.

I know it might sound unimportant to the general population, but to many adoptees, it's very important. Every new mother feels something she never felt before when her baby is born. I now understand there was an added dimension for me, although I didn't realize it at the time and was unable to express it. Part of the bond I had with my son was that I could see something in him of myself. And that was totally new to me. It's something the majority of people in life just take for granted.

Being pregnant with Dustin and experiencing the awesomeness of carrying and delivering my son, was the catalyst to begin a serious search for my natural mother.

First Steps in Searching

The first step I took was to go to an ALMA meeting. (ALMA is an acronym for Adoptees Liberty Movement Association.) The closest meeting was in Philadelphia at a Unitarian church, which was about an hour from where we were living. A few months pregnant and emotional about preparing to search, I attended the meeting with my husband. I didn't realize the significance of this at the time, but the speaker that day was Florence Fisher. She is well-known as the foremother of the adoptee rights movement. I was absolutely mesmerized as she spoke.

During the meeting people would periodically leave the audience when called, and go back and sit in a circle with those who would assist them personally with their search. A man named David Martini and his wife helped me. They asked me if I knew my original name. When I told them yes, they were absolutely delighted. They gave me excellent search tips and recommended going in person to the Children's Home Society to find out more information about my history. They cautioned me above all else to tell CHS nothing that I already knew, and particularly to never tell them that I knew my original name. They said CHS would tell me much less if they knew that I knew my name. I took careful note.

The Martini's advice was right on target. Over the years, it's probably the number one piece of search advice I would give anyone. When you are dealing with the holders of your information, whether it's agencies, social workers, etc., it's best to never tell them what you already know. People often tell you more when they think you don't know anything. You will often find out more by asking a question, then being quiet and just taking in what people say. Once they say it, write it down, so you don't forget and you remember the information accurately.

Later on in the week I was in prayer about everything and I felt God speak to me that all I needed was my name. He also reassured me that I would reunite with my original mother. I didn't just take careful note of this in my heart. I wrote it all out, for myself and for my natural mother.

All through the years I had been writing a book for my natural mother. I hoped to give it to her someday. It was a book of letters that were from my heart to hers, telling her my feelings over the years of how much I had thought of her, missed her, and longed to see her and tell her many things.

Larry and I made the appointment to go to Richmond and meet with the Children's Home Society and find out what we could.

Maybe I was about to finally look into the face that looked like mine.

Chapter 3—
Search and Reunion...
Or Maybe Not

"Not to have knowledge of what happened before you were born is to be condemned to live forever as a child."

— *Cicero*

I established a relationship with God from the time I was a child. I have never had any problem with my identity in Christ, or accepting God as my Father. I not only accepted Him, I talked to Him constantly all throughout the day. This is what the Bible refers to as "praying without ceasing." It simply means, ongoing conversation with God all the time.

I mention this because when adopted people begin to explore their biological identity, they are often admonished, "Just find your identity in Christ." Knowing your identity in Christ and knowing the identity of your earthly parents are two totally different things.

It matters a whole lot to non-adopted people who their parents are and where they come from. They celebrate it all the time. The discussion of genetic mirroring, "Oh, the baby looks just like Aunt Frances when she was a baby!" The family reunions. Family trees. The fact that Ancestry.com recently sold for 1.6 billion dollars and has two million subscribers. There's a reason for all of this. Family matters!

When talking with non-adoptees, many seem to have an idea that family matters... unless you're adopted and speaking of your natural family. Then you're just a bad adoptee whose adoption "didn't work out." This is an unfortunate stereotype, and it's not true.

Going Back to Go Forward

I always wanted to know the truth of my history. I had courage to express this as a teenager. With the blessing of my adoptive parents, I wrote a letter to CHS requesting non-identifying information. I received a few short paragraphs back with basic details that were appreciated, but left me with even more questions.

n 1990, Larry and I made a visit to the Children's Home Society of Virginia.

I still remember how cold the room was as we waited. How I snuggled next to Larry, not just for physical warmth even though it was summer time, but just wanting comfort.

I still remember the sound of the social worker's heels clicking in the hallway as she rounded the corner and came into the room with my file.

I remember how she opened the folder and carefully read what she could share with us. She read slowly, so as to not divulge anything she wasn't supposed to. It was all non-identifying but she had no idea I had my original name. I kept that knowledge carefully guarded. I could have never found my original family simply based upon the information the social worker gave me. However, the non-identifying information proved to be helpful when I utilized it along with my original name.

Larry was frustrated.

He told me afterwards that he wanted to go over to the desk, knock the lady out—as nice as she was—and take the file. He was so tired of me not having my personal information—the basic knowledge of my history.

Perhaps there is nothing so puzzling for adult adoptees than the fact that in a closed adoption you are not permitted to see the information about YOU, however total strangers are allowed to sit at their desks and read all of YOUR information.

Tears would quickly spring forth as the social worker shared from the files...things like, "The baby's mother came to visit today. She held her but she was asleep the whole time. She was disappointed that the baby was asleep and wants to come back and see her when she's awake. She is struggling with relinquishment."

That broke my heart, and excited me at the same time. I took it as a guarantee that my mother would want to reunite.

My mother struggled with giving me up!

She wanted to see me again before she relinquished me.

It was just a matter of time before we would be face-to-face again!

The Reunion Program

After getting all of the non-identifying information I could, the social worker asked if I would like to be a part of their reunion program.

I jumped at the chance. Knowing what I now know, I sometimes regret that, realizing I could have searched on my own with a different outcome. Thinking they had all the information at their fingertips and it would be an easy search, versus me trying on my own, I said yes.

My birth state (Virginia) is currently a closed state, so that means I have no rights there to receive my Original Birth Certificate (OBC). At the time of this writing, adoptees only have equal rights without compromises in seven states.

I believe it is important to note that a birth certificate is just that, a certificate of birth, not a certificate of adoption. Therefore, does it not make sense that it should reflect the correct information of birth? This is just one area in adoption that desperately needs reform.

The court was petitioned to open my records to a confidential intermediary (CI), from the agency.

Once the CI found my mother, she would find out her wishes and then serve as a go-between for our reunion... or not.

The CI was very likeable. Each day I lived in anticipation of hearing about her search progress.

Excitement and Then... Devastation

The day came when the confidential intermediary called and said she had found my mother. I was so excited I could hardly stand it.

She shared with my mother that I had turned out well and had become a minister. "You'd be so proud of her," the CI said.

Immediately my mother responded, "I'm sure I'd be very proud of her, but she wouldn't be very proud of me."

Ugh.

I steadied myself, listening to the CI talk as she explained that my mother "felt unworthy of being found..." and "struggled with some life circumstances that she could not face me with..."

My legs almost gave out from under me when the CI dropped the news that my mother had decided she did not want to reunite.

The room was spinning.

This can't be real, I thought.

It has to be a mistake.

She will change her mind once she's had more time...

I even pinched myself to make sure it wasn't a nightmare.

Surely I was asleep.

This might happen to other people, but not to me, right?

A few days later, I realized it was reality.

I begged the CI to let me write her a letter explaining my feelings, one that did not contain any identifying information. I've always been able to reach people's hearts through writing. I had hopes, if I could just communicate with her, even without revealing our identities, it would work out.

The CI said this was against the rules.

The 30-Day Wait

My mother was given 30 days to change her mind.

I prayed.

I fasted.

I travailed.

I believed.

I worshipped.

I cried.

I named it.

I claimed it.

I blabbed it.

I grabbed it.

I bound it.

I loosed it.

I pleaded the blood.

I did a Jericho march.

I waved my white hanky.

I anointed it.

I declared it.

I spoke to the mountain.

I called down fire.

I called down rain.

But at the end of the 30 days she told the CI that her decision was still no.

I couldn't imagine it.

This was really happening.

Didn't God say?

Was I incapable of hearing from Him anymore?

Even though I had clearly and unmistakably heard His voice all throughout my life. Despite the fact that I had ministered in the gifts of the spirit and been clearly on target time and time again.

God said I would reunite with my mother.

He spoke that to me as clearly as when He spoke to me to go into the ministry!

But she said, "no," and the case—with the agency and the Henrico County Court System, was closed.

It seemed as though I really missed Him on this one.

After this, as I was in personal prayer or as I ministered to others, I relentlessly checked everything over and over and over again to ensure that I thought I was hearing from God, now struggling with doubt. While previously bold, I was now afraid to speak out about what God spoke to me. Because I had begun to fear that I was now incapable of hearing Him at all.

No Second Chances

I was informed by the CI that due to the volume of cases, there were no do-overs even if my mother changed her mind later.

For whatever reason, the CI did tell her that my name was changed and was now Deanna.

And she also told me that I had a brother and a sister.

It was unfathomable to me that I wouldn't know my brother and sister.

My mind was racing with the ramifications of what her "no" meant, not just for me but for others. My brother, my sister, my own children!

Getting the final call from the CI that my mother had declined was the worst day of my life, up to that time. There is nothing like the feeling an adoptee experiences when their mother says no to reunion. In the adoptee community, this is referred to as "secondary rejection." Absolutely nothing can compare to it. I've spoken to adoptees that this has happened to and every one of them describes secondary rejection as a searing pain beyond any realm of description.

Moving Right Along...

During the time of the CI's call with the news, Larry and I were in the process of making a transition to serve as youth and music pastors of a larger church, Gospel Temple Assembly of God, in Dayton, Ohio. We said

goodbye to the Viscontis but it was never really goodbye.
We weren't just staff members. We had become family.
To this day we still visit regularly, preach in one
another's churches, and our children know us as Uncle
Randy and Aunt Dawn and Uncle Larry and Aunt
Deanna.

After experiencing the secondary rejection of my natural
mother, I cried myself to sleep almost every night for two
years. I had my faith, the church, my husband and
children, and friends. But I was not in community with
any adoptees who could understand first-hand what I was
going through. I was missing the comfort and wisdom of
those who had walked the same road.

I worked myself to exhaustion every day, balancing my
role as youth pastor's wife, mother of two babies who
were just a year apart, and music pastor—overseeing a
large music department/worship program. I was
exhausted and I liked it that way. Work has always been
one of my two drugs of choice, food being the other. It
was my long standing habit to work myself to exhaustion
in an effort to prove my worth and now I had the perfect
opportunity in a demanding role with larger
responsibilities that included worship programming and
leading, directing full scale musicals, and co-pastoring a
youth group—all while caring full-time for two babies.
Church work can provide the perfect merry-go-round to
let you think you're escaping from pain.

But every night I had to go to sleep.

And when everything around me stopped I would lay
awake, stare at the ceiling into the dark and think about

the fact that the person who birthed me—my mother, didn't want to see me, meet me, look at me or talk to me.

Having two babies myself, I couldn't wrap my brain around it. How was this possible? Even the scriptures declare, "Can a mother forget the baby at her breast and have no compassion on the child she has borne?" –Isaiah 49:15.

Tears would course down my cheeks and run into my ears as I gently rubbed my feet together to soothe myself to sleep, as I've done all my life.

I would do this night after night until sleep came, longing for the busyness of morning much more than the hard reality of the night.

Two years went by.

The Day the Tide Turned

One day I was having lunch with Norma Hartman, another of our pastors on staff, and she asked me why I wasn't still pursuing the search.

I thought this was the craziest thing I had ever heard.

My mother said no.

Norma said, "Have you prayed about it?"

I don't know why I didn't think of this before.

Was it such a bizarre question after all?

Norma knew I was still hurting and crying myself to sleep every night for two years. I was hiding it very well at church, but occasionally I shared my feelings with those close to me whom I trusted. That day after our lunch, the two of us went into the sanctuary and prayed.

As we were praying, God spoke to me very clearly.

No, not in an audible voice.

I don't know anyone personally who has heard Him that way.

I heard him in the same way He always deals with me, in the still small voice in my spirit, just as with Elijah in the Bible.

Him: "Did she tell YOU no, directly?"

Me: "No. She didn't tell ME directly."

Him: "Did I tell you no?"

Me: "Well no, you actually told me I would reunite with her and I'm a little confused right now by what's happened... it's pretty much freaking me out that I can't hear from You at all anymore and maybe if I'm wrong on this, I could also be wrong about so much more that I've always believed..."

Him: "Let me clear up the confusion for you. She didn't tell YOU no. She told someone else no. She told a stranger to both of you no. And most of all, I didn't tell you no. I never told you to stop moving forward on this, Deanna."

Me: "So, you're actually telling me... yes?"

Him: "Of course. I never told you no. I never told you to stop. You have your name, that's all you need. I told you that from the beginning. Now, go and find her."

Well, if God says, "yes,"—no one can stop it!

Don't flesh-and-blood have a right to talk to one another without interference?

Maybe not a right in the eyes of the State, but a right in the eyes of God?

What kind of law prevents a daughter from speaking directly to her mother?

I believe these are unnatural laws.

Void of the justice of God... of compassion.

Let's Try This Again

I left the sanctuary that day, went home and started my search again, with my original name, the one I had found in the box under the bed.

It was the early 1990s. There was no Internet, and searching was different then. Larry and I were living on a meager salary at the time. Being financially tight with two little babies required me to be very careful with what I spent. Some months my search budget was only five or ten dollars. My search was conducted through regular US Mail, libraries, city directories, and long distance phone calls. There were no e-mails or all-inclusive long distance plans. Sometimes my entire budget for the month was taken up on just a few long distance phone calls and I had to wait until the next month to do more.

I rarely had time to watch TV, but because I had the flu I was watching a talk show featuring a private investigator named Joseph J. Culligan. They were promoting his book, *You, Too, Can Find Anybody.* I was intrigued by the book. The show featured testimonials of people who were using his techniques to find people for as little as eight dollars! All of it was through public information and was perfectly legal.

Since I was sick, I asked Larry if he could pick up the book from the store at the mall. He left right away, while I was still watching the show, and went to B. Dalton Books at the Dayton Mall. The employee at the store said they were sold out of the book. Larry left the store and was already several stores away when the same employee came running after him and said, "Sir, I can't understand how this happened...it's the strangest thing ever, but when I went back to the cash register, a copy of the book was laying right there on top!"

We knew who put the book there. :)

Shout now, somebody!

I started following all the principles of the book for my search. In short order I had tried everything in the book except for two things.

The first thing was the instruction to contact the Salvation Army, who would find your family member for just ten dollars. Specifically, Joe Culligan's book said this:

The Salvation Army has a very competent and experienced missing persons bureau. They will conduct a search for you to find a father, mother, brother, sister, son or daughter. The fee is just ten dollars. Contact the local Salvation Army listed in the White Pages of your telephone book.

I didn't think that could possibly work. I had huge doubts about it, so I tried all the other things in the book first that seemed more plausible.

The second thing was to order the Social Security Death Master File. I had checked into it but all the places I contacted were more than I could pay at the time.

I got discouraged and wrote Joseph Culligan a letter, just to vent.

Imagine my surprise when I was napping with the babies one day and the phone rang and I picked it up and it was him! He called to encourage me. "There is such determination in your letter," he said. "It's not a matter of if you're going to succeed, it's when! Please keep going." He also told me the main thing I needed to do was the Social Security Death Master File.

I didn't bother to tell him I didn't have the money. I didn't think he'd understand.

I thanked him profusely for taking the time to call and care about me and my situation.

I lay in bed crying myself to sleep that night as was my custom, and felt prompted to read the book again, so I did. I noticed the part about the Salvation Army and had an overwhelming urge that I was supposed to call them.

I called the next morning at nine. A kind woman answered and I asked her if they find family members for ten dollars. She said that under the right circumstances they do. (I'm not sure if they still do this, I am sharing what my experience was back then.)

I said, "What are the right circumstances?"

She said, "Well, first let me ask...are you adopted?"

Ugh.

I was always honest during my search, even when asked the hard questions like this. I usually just prayed that they wouldn't ask them!

I said, "Yes ma'am, I am."

"Well, then our services in this regard are not for you," she said.

"I figured as much but I just thought it didn't hurt to ask."

She inquired further about my situation, saying she would still like to help if she could. She already knew I was adopted and still wanted to help. This was amazing!

After sharing with her where I was in my search she said, "I would recommend the Social Security Death Master File as a means to get your information." I told her I wanted to do that but was looking for an affordable way to get it. She said, "Let me give you the number of a friend who can help," and provided me a person's name in California.

When I called the person in California they gave me what I needed for thirteen dollars.

Yes, THIRTEEN DOLLARS!!

Shout now, somebody!

Finding the Living through the Dead

My Death Master File information came from California by US mail in a few days.

One way to find living people is by first finding dead people whose paper trail leads you to them. Men rarely change their last names, but women usually do if and when they marry. So, I zeroed in on finding my grandfather in order to find my mother. It's ironic that it would be my grandfather that would lead to my mother since he's the one who kicked her out of the house when she was pregnant with me! I just had to laugh. ~~This is what you call Pentecostal Karma.~~

There were hundreds of names of men on the list. I ordered copies all of their obituaries from the public library and had to wait for them by US mail.

I compared the information on each obit with the non-identifying information I received from the agency. Things like my grandparents' occupations, the number of brothers and sisters my mother had, and the family's religious background. If a man was Catholic or a chemist, or had three children, I knew he wasn't my grandfather.

The point came where I was waiting for one last obituary.

One.

I had one chance left to find my grandfather, using the Death Master File.

I'm going to try not to preach here, ~~I am usually not successful at that!~~ but my friends... there are times things are right down to the wire... you think you have one last hope... and maybe you even think all hope is gone...............

HOLD ON!!!

DO. NOT. GIVE. UP.

The very last obituary to land in my mailbox fit my grandfather's description exactly, except the number of his children was off by one. I wondered if one of his children could have passed away before he did. My thought was if so, the same funeral home was more than likely utilized by the family.

The funeral home listed was the Woody Funeral Home in Richmond. I called and asked to speak with someone who could talk with me about a previous funeral. They connected me with an assistant who was so helpful. It's important to note that they shared information that was made public, and none of what was disclosed to me was unlawful.

I asked if this man had a son whose funeral was conducted there, previously. Upon checking, the files, she confirmed that was the case.

This WAS my grandfather!

Hello... I Love You, Won't You Tell Me Your Name?

Now, I needed to figure out which of the children listed was my mother. I already knew from the non-identifying information received from the agency that my mother was the youngest of her siblings. The assistant explained to me that children are listed on obituaries from oldest to youngest. I realized she would be the last child listed on the obituary, and since she was no longer a child at the time of his death it bore her current (married) name at the time.

I will never forget being on the phone with that assistant, hearing her say my mother's name. "Oh my," I said, voice faltering, "you've just told me my mother's name."

"I'm just doing my job," she said.

"No, no, no, you don't understand," I cried. "I've never known my mother's name before."

Once I discovered her name through the funeral home obituary, I called information to get her phone number and used other means of public information to get her address.

There was no such thing as caller ID at the time, only the old kind of answering machines that gave no information on who was calling. I discovered her name and phone number in the afternoon and hoped she was still at work. I called and listened to the message on her answering machine.

It was her voice.

I listened to the message fifteen or more times, sobbing at the sound of my mother's voice for the first time, as an adult. I kept dialing the number again and again, listening and crying.

Larry walked in the door with an evangelist friend he had been out with for the afternoon. (I didn't call him because cell phones didn't exist at the time.) As soon as he saw me he knew what had happened without me saying a word. I was so overcome with emotion, he just knew.

He turned to the evangelist friend and said, "My wife has just found her mother."

He stood in the living room and held me as I cried in his arms while our friend asked why in the world I had never known who my mother was.

Larry explained while I dried my tears and ran off to start working.

There was no time to stand there bawling all day.

We spent several hours packing the van and buckled the babies into their car seats.

Then, I had one more call to make.

This time she picked up the phone.

I heard her say, "Hello," and I immediately hung up.

Turning to Larry, I said, "She's home. Let's go."

We buckled our seat belts, pulled out of the driveway, and proceeded to drive for eight hours.

I was determined to show up unannounced on her doorstep to tell her that she was worthy of being found.

Chapter 4—
"Hi Mom, I'm Home!"

"In all of us there is a hunger, marrow deep, to know our heritage, to know who we are and where we have come from. Without this enriching knowledge, there is a hollow yearning. No matter what our attainments in life, there is a vacuum, an emptiness and a most disquieting loneliness!"

— *Alex Haley*

I made the phone call just before we left Dayton to hear her voice live, and make sure she wasn't away on vacation or anything. I'm a detail person. ~~Okay, a control freak. Whatever.~~

We drove eight hours through the night to get to Richmond. Before we arrived at our hotel I asked Larry to drive by the Henrico County Courthouse as well as the Children's Home Society. Both had declared my case closed. Both were the "powers that be"—the ones who held the authority to make the decisions regarding me.

But I wasn't a baby anymore.

I was a fully empowered woman.

I had taken control and found my natural mother without their permission.

I could talk to her if I wanted to, and they couldn't stop me.

I was proud of myself. It was a hard search and I never gave up. The powers that be said, "Case closed."

I said, "CASE OPEN!"

Praise Break on the Lawn

Larry did just as I asked and drove to the courthouse. It was the wee hours of the morning and no one was there when we pulled up. It wasn't about an audience. For me it was what it represented. When we got to the courthouse, I got out of the car, stood on the front lawn and had my own praise break. ~~T.D. Jakes would have been proud~~.

I got back into the car feeling so much adrenaline and said, "Okay, drive to CHS!"

Larry looked at me and said, "You are the craziest woman I know!"

He shook his head and drove on to CHS.

It's of note that Larry's nickname for me all these years has been, "Sassy."

A Divine Appointment

We pulled into Motel 6, which was what we could afford at the time, and Larry went in to get a room. I stayed in the car with the boys. While waiting, I noticed a man standing on the sidewalk in front of our car. I rolled down my window and called out to him, asking if he was from Richmond. He said he did not live there currently but knew the area well. I asked him if he knew where the street was located that my mother lived on.

Larry is great with directions but I was so eager to find out how to get there, I wanted to ask someone before he even looked up the directions.

The man introduced himself as Craig and gave me directions to get to the street my mother lived on. Then he asked why we were in town. I told him, giving him the basic outline of everything I've just written. He was blown away by the story and kept asking me more questions, seeming genuinely excited for me.

I asked him why he was in town. He said he was there to do a radio show but didn't give many other details. I mentioned how cool I thought that was that he was doing a show and wished him success. Larry came out with our room key and I wrapped up the conversation with Craig and went to get settled with the family. I explained to Larry about our exchange and also how to get to my mother's place.

The conversation with Craig would later prove to be an absolutely astounding twist in the trip to Richmond.

Getting Ready

Moments after walking into our room, my family conked out completely. They slept most of the day they were so tired. I stayed awake the entire day. Actually I never slept a wink for the next 48 hours.

I had waited my whole life for this.

I showered, put make-up on and dressed, styled my hair and changed outfits at least five times. I was so nervous, and I'm not typically nervous about what I'm going to wear, how I'm going to look or what I'm going to say, but this was a once-in-a-lifetime-moment.

Finally, I settled on one outfit. Pink. High heels. My hair was like a mane at the time. It was so long it went half way down my back. No, this was not due to being Pentecostal. It just happened to be my style at the time, and besides that, my husband loved it. I usually pulled sections of it up in little bows or scrunchies, this night being no exception. I swept some of my long curly locks up into a pink bow, and dabbed on my favorite perfume.

I was twenty-seven-years-old.

The Plan

I had no idea what I was going to say when I knocked on her door. No idea at all. When I prayed about it, God said, "I'm going to give you the words just at the time you need them."

Being a Pentecostal girl, I was okay with that. ~~God gives us words on the fly.~~

Some friends who knew I was going to do this just couldn't accept that I was waiting until the moment to decide what to say. They said, "What do you mean you don't know what you're going to say? That's crazy! You have to plan this!"

I jokingly said, "I dunno, maybe I'll knock and yell, 'Hi Mom! I'm home!'"

Why didn't I just call her and talk to her by phone instead of showing up?

Lots of people have since asked me that.

I didn't want to take the chance of not being able to see her at least once.

I had to see my mother.

I had to.

I needed to look into her face, with the capacity to remember it—at least once in my lifetime. And with a phone call there was no guarantee of that. I wanted to see her face, needed to see her... longed to do that, just one time.

I had no plan after that, or an expectation.

I was not going to keep calling or writing or contacting her.

I needed one meeting.

Just one.

I often told Larry, "Once this is accomplished, this part of me will settle down inside. I promise."

He was so hoping for that.

As we get further into the story, I'll share if that was reality—if I actually settled down inside, or not.

I promised never to publicize my natural mother's name in my writing, therefore to honor that promise, I call her Judy in my writing. In keeping with that I will also refer to her husband as Tom. (Neither of their real names.)

My plan was to meet Judy once, say what I had to say, give her the book I wrote to her to keep if she wanted it, and then ask her if I could have one photo to remember her by if she never wanted to see me again. I took a camera just in case she was not willing to part with a photo.

I believe every human being has a right to look into the eyes of the two people they originate from, at least once. If they are not still alive—a name and a photo of the persons they come from. I don't believe they have a right to bombard them after that with further contact, to stalk or harass them. I do, however, believe that if you birth a child, it's the humane thing, the kind thing—yes, the right thing, to give them a face-to-face with you at least once, if they request it.

A Walk to Remember

My husband said I didn't have to do this alone, but I knew I had to.

He and the boys waited in the car.

Judy and I had started out just the two of us in 1966, and that's how I wanted this moment to be.

To me, this was sacred.

I exited the car and headed toward her door, legs like Jello with every step.

I felt a power other than mine carry me up the walk.

I knocked.

She opened the door and smiled.

She had no idea who I was.

"Judy?"

"Yes..." she nodded.

"Judy, please don't be afraid...but my name is Deanna and I think you know who I am."

She stared at me and I stared back at her.

We were frozen in time, standing for what seemed like forever, just gazing.

After a few moments I broke the silence and asked if I could come in.

She looked away, threw one hand up in the air and said, "Well, it's better than standing on the porch."

Turning quickly on her heel, she led me through the living room to her kitchen.

I assumed she was inviting me to sit. Steadying myself I took a seat at the small wooden kitchen table. She flitted back and forth from the sink to the stove and busied herself while she talked non-stop. She began making coffee, running water in the sink, all the while, hands shaking.

Wiping down water drops on the counter with paper towels...

Taking two mugs out of the cabinet...

The entire time, I sensed God's guiding presence, His grace carrying me.

He spoke to me to say nothing. "Be silent," He said. "Don't speak until she exhausts all that she has to say. Then, and only then...you speak."

She began with, "I know you don't understand...you don't understand my decisions. Why I gave you up, why I said no to reunion two years ago, why I did a lot of things..."

Pausing for a moment she said, "Oh my God, you look just like your father. He was Greek. I called him a Greek God..."

She stared at me another few moments.

And she went on for about twenty minutes to list all of her perceived failures.

After giving the litany of her shortcomings as she saw them, fully spent of all her words, she finished it off by telling me I would be very sorry that I found her.

"You haven't found anything... you've found nothing," she said, blankly staring and shaking her head.

Then she waited to hear what I had to say.

Chapter 5— A Not-So-Ordinary Coffee Chat

"We shall not cease our explorations, and the end of our exploring will be to arrive back where we started and know the place for the first time."

— *T.S. Eliot*

Folding my hands on my lap, I gently and inconspicuously rubbed my fingers together as is my habit when unsure of what's next.

Once she poured out everything she had to say, I rested my hand on the coffee cup in front of me, swirling my index finger gently on the rim, looked square into her eyes and said, "I knew you felt this way two years ago, when you talked to the confidential intermediary. You shared what you perceived as your failures with her and you felt I wouldn't be proud of you. You said that you weren't worthy of being found. But the truth is this— whether you've failed at certain things or you haven't failed but just think you have—none of it matters to me. Because the fact is, we've all failed. I've failed. I'm sure I will again. And I've gone through hell and back to find you. And I'd do it all again just to be sitting here with you. Because to God, and to me—you're worthy of being found."

Silence.

She stared at me for a moment.

Took it all in.

Then she got up, walked over to my side of the table, and wrapped both arms around my head.

She began to cry from a very deep place.

Not your typical cry, something more like a wail.

She had me in a headlock of sorts, arms gathered around my thick mane of hair...cradling the pink bow on top, choking through sobs...

"You're beautiful.

You're beautiful...

I don't know what I've done to deserve a second chance, but you're beautiful. You're beautiful."

Over and over again she said it as she cried from a place fathomless to many, understood only by her fellow first mothers. Those who have experienced what it is like to lose the child they carried in their body for nine months and birthed—and relinquished.

People ask me, "What were you thinking when she was saying and doing all of that?"

My overriding thought was, "She's not kicking me out. I'm still here."

The whole time I was sitting in her kitchen chair my thoughts kept racing back to think, "I haven't been asked to leave yet. This is incredible!"

Even today, at this moment, it's amazing to me.

The fascination of sitting in my mother's kitchen with her for the first time never, ever leaves.

I can call up the moment instantly, twenty years later and remember it, just as it was.

And still, even as I type these words, the tears flow uncontrollably down my face.

I taste the coffee, with cream and sugar.

Feel my hands on the table.

Her arms around my head.

Warm tears falling in wavy locks of hair.

The sounds of her crying in my ear.

Glancing over and noticing the peanut butter crackers on the counter were the same exact brand that I eat all the time. Pretty much every day.

I noticed how alike our hands are and how we reach for the warm cup of coffee as we speak.

I noticed how she says, "you know," a lot, and how I do the same.

I noticed how we both tighten our lips at the end of a sentence and keep them like that while we're thinking.

I tried profusely to burn it all in my mind quickly, never to forget it.

How much time would we have together before she would ask me to leave, with only memories left for the remainder of my lifetime?

Headlock released and using a paper towel to dry the tears, she took the spot across from me at the table and we began talking again.

I learned more about my brother and sister. She pointed to two large portraits on the living room wall. I locked my eyes on them and never wanted to look away, as staring into their faces I saw parts of my own. I felt a warm wave come over my being, something I can't really describe with mere words at the recognition of parts of my own face reflected in someone else... my siblings.

Suddenly she was startled, interrupting my love fest with the sibling portraits and said, "Oh my! Tom is going to be calling any moment!"

"Who's Tom?" I asked.

She explained that Tom was her boyfriend. After enduring an abusive marriage to my siblings' father for several decades, she had divorced around the time the CI had contacted her. Going through a difficult divorce was just one reason she felt overwhelmed and a failure at the time.

She and Tom had been dating for a while but had no plans for anything more serious. Both had their share of deep hurts in the past, and because of this, wanted companionship but feared marriage.

I wondered if I was a secret from Tom.

I asked her, "Does he know about me?"

She said that Tom did know all about me, in fact he would know me as Melanie.

I was surprised.

Shocked, in fact.

Sure enough, almost immediately after she spoke of Tom, the phone rang. He was calling to check on her before bedtime.

I wondered if she would share with him that I was there. I didn't have to wonder long.

Right away she said, "Tom, there's someone here with me."

"This late at night?" he said. "Who would that be?"

"I'll give you a hint...she's twenty-seven."

"Twenty-seven? Who do we know that's twenty-seven?"

[Tears]

"Melanie's here, Tom. It's Melanie."

"Oh my God," he said. "I'll be right there."

Chapter 6—
Never Can Say Goodbye

"The past isn't dead. It isn't even the past."

— *William Faulkner*

Tom walked through the door no less than ten minutes after the phone call.

I had no idea what to expect but I was pleasantly surprised when he strode across the room, embraced me, and said, "I'm so glad you've come. I think she's needed this."

From the first second I met Tom, I was absolutely crazy about him.

The three of us sat and began to talk and Tom said, "Deanna, you have a family...correct?"

I said, "Oh yes, I have a husband and two children." He asked where they were. I said, "Ummmmm... actually they are out in the car..."

"All this time?" said Judy, eyes wide with alarm.

"Yes," I said, "all this time." ~~My husband was about to pee his pants.~~

Judy expressed fear about meeting Larry and the boys. She thought they would be angry with her because she had said no to reunion several years before. "They aren't angry with you," I said. "My husband has come all this way with me in hopes of meeting you. And trust me, the boys are going to love you too!"

"Oh my..." said Judy nervously. "I can't believe they've been out there all along. Bring them in, please bring them in."

Judy has no other grandchildren by birth, and this would be her first time to lay eyes on the oldest two. (Savanna Rose wasn't born yet. We reunited in 1993 and Savanna Rose didn't arrive until 1997.) Jordan was two-years-old—still in diapers the night of our reunion, and Dustin was three.

I went outside and asked my husband and the boys to come in. Larry walked in, greeted Judy, and said, "Thank you for my wife." She swallowed tearfully, at a loss for words.

The boys came running in the house, so glad to be released from the confines of the car. They skipped around in circles in the living room. I was afraid all their running around was going to rattle Judy and Tom. It didn't. She stood there crying and wringing her hands, saying, "They are the most beautiful children in the world. Let them run!"

After Larry returned from the restroom we all sat down in the living room. Well, the boys were still doing their share of running around, but in short order Tom corralled them off to the side and had them engaged in a game. This left Larry and I to focus on conversation with Judy.

After some discussion about my brother and sister and other family, I asked about my father. She reaffirmed that he was someone she dated who was Greek and had dark hair, like mine. She shared that he refused to acknowledge his part in my existence, and when she told him about the pregnancy, he gave her no help at all.

I began to share with her what the adoption agency had told me in the non-identifying information about my father. Quickly she interrupted, telling me that she had lied to them about who he was. She said I would find nothing by pursuing my non-identifying information in that regard because she gave them false information so that no one would know his true identity.

"So he's not your coworker from the drug store?" I asked. (The non-identifying information said she had worked with my father at a drug store, and this was how they met.)

"No, I lied to them about that," she said flatly, eyes glancing down at the floor.

I asked her about my original birth certificate, and she said she lied on the paperwork for that as well. She told me if I was ever to receive my OBC it wouldn't be correct anyway, so it was useless to pursue it.

In a bizarre twist, she said my natural father had contacted her in recent years after her divorce, with phone calls she considered to be harassing in nature. According to her, he continued to refuse to accept my existence, acting as if nothing had ever happened. I asked her what the purpose of the calls was, and she said he had heard about her divorce and called her, possibly wanting to know if she was available. She was so angry about the phone calls, she said she had thought of "bringing him up on charges" as she put it, and had gone so far as to consult an attorney but been advised it would do her no good to pursue it.

My emotional intelligence was in overdrive every time the subject of my father arose. When verbalizing anything remotely connected to him, her eyes would suddenly enlarge and she'd quickly look away, or put her hands up, as if constructing a boundary between us. There appeared to be an insurmountable invisible wall that had been established when it came to the subject of my father.

I was so grateful to be sitting there with Judy and Tom, I didn't push it. I also hoped to meet my brother and sister soon, and didn't want to mess anything up.

After several hours of conversation, and getting as much information as I could about my background to the point to which Judy was willing to go, I got to the heart of what would be the most important decision of the evening, aside from her initial decision to let me come inside.

It was well after midnight when I said, "Judy, I've come all this way, with one intention—to do exactly what we did tonight. I'm not here to make your life difficult, or ask for anything materially. I promise you this. Now, the choice from here on is yours. We have a hotel here in Richmond and we've taken some time off to be here. We can spend time with you as you are able to this week, or you can make a decision to have some space and think about it for a while. You can contact me later and let me know your wishes going forward. I can be a once-a-year phone call, a Christmas card, or you can never see me again if that's what you want. We can develop our relationship further, or you can decide that ongoing contact with me is not for you. I will respect that. I just needed what we have experienced tonight—to look into your face once in my life when I could remember it, have this conversation and also give you this." I presented her with the book I wrote for her and continued, "I would like a photo of you to keep if you decide this is our final conversation."

Before she could answer Tom spoke up and said, "Well that's ridiculous! We're all having dinner together tomorrow night!"

I smiled, warmed by his words.

But it needed to be Judy's decision. I said, "Judy, I appreciate what Tom has said, but the decision is yours. Please, think about it further, and let me know your desire."

With gentleness in her voice she said, "Let's meet tomorrow night."

She went on to say she was sorry we had to get a motel room.

"Please, stay here," she said. "I don't want you to have to get a room after coming all this way."

I let her know how touched we were by her offer but said we wanted to give her space, and were fine at the hotel.

It was getting late. As much as I would have loved to have stayed all night to talk with them, we made plans for dinner at a local restaurant at five pm the next night.

Judy and Tom walked us back out to the van. When Larry and I put the boys in the car seats I was getting ready to get in on my side of the van when Judy grabbed me and held on to me for dear life. She stood beside the van, arms clenched around me firmly, as she alternated between crying and a low humming in my ear as I looked up at the night sky, more tears falling.

I wasn't sure what she was thinking and I didn't want to assume anything, so I asked.

"Are you okay?"

"No, I'm not okay," she said. "I'm afraid you're not going to come back tomorrow."

"There's no way that's going to happen," I assured her. "I didn't search for years to the ends of the earth to find you and drive eight hours and knock on your door to not come back tomorrow! I promise you, I will be right back here tomorrow as soon as you get home from work."

She held me again, weeping.

"I hear what you're saying," she said. "But the last time I said goodbye, I didn't see you again, until now..."

Chapter 7—
Getting to Know You

"I think we dream so we don't have to be apart for so long. If we're in each other's dreams, we can be together all the time."

— *A.A. Milne,* Winnie the Pooh

True to my word, I never asked Judy for anything. In fact, prior to February 26, 2013, I never asked her for even one thing.

Even so, on the night we were reunited, she made the kind gesture to give me several photos of my sister and brother. I was absolutely fascinated by seeing their faces in photos though we had not spoken yet.

Sleepless in Richmond

Larry and I got the boys settled at the motel and he went to sleep.

I never slept. The entire night.

I would turn the light off and shut my eyes but shortly thereafter I would turn on the lamp beside the bed and look at my brother and sister's photos.

I had never spoken to them. But I loved them already.

Larry would wince each time the light went back on and I could tell it was disturbing his sleep greatly so I'd apologize for looking at my pictures again.

"That's okay babe, look at your pictures as many times as you need to..."

He would roll over and try his best to go back to sleep every few minutes.

I love that man. My heart becomes flooded with emotions I can't even fully express when I remember moments like that. Moments where he just understood what many people who aren't adopted have so much of a problem getting. Times when he cared about what was important to me, rather than what was convenient for him.

By this time I had not slept for 48 hours. My family woke up and found me already up, showered and ready to go.

Judy had worked at the company where she was employed for many years. I think at the time it was close to fifteen years or more. She had dutifully headed off to work that morning.

An Unexpected Letter

Our family was getting ready to run some errands before breakfast and we went outside to our car. I was surprised to see a white piece of paper tucked underneath the windshield wipers.

"It's a note from Judy," I thought. My first reaction was that maybe she had thought it over in the middle of the night and changed her mind about dinner and about ongoing contact. I was bracing myself for this change. My heart was pounding much faster as I took the note out from under the wipers and began to read.

"What is it, babe?" Larry quickly said.

My heart was relieved as I read the note from the man I'd chatted with yesterday:

> *Deanna,*
>
> *Your story was fascinating. I want to hear the rest of it! Come and tell me how things went with your mother.*
>
> *Craig*
>
> *Room 103*

I told Larry I wanted to go talk to Craig before we left for our errands in case he wasn't there when we got back. So we got in the car and swung around to motel room 103 and could see in the window that Craig was sitting at the table in his room eating a bowl of cereal. The curtain was pulled back and he saw us as we drove up.

I asked Larry if he wanted to come in with me and he
said since the boys were in their car seats and Craig had
the window open where he could see us, it would be
okay. People who knew my boys at that age can attest,
they were such a handful, especially Jordan who was
hyperactive, and it would have been much more of a
challenge to get them out of the car to go in. They were
occupied with books and toys and snacks for a time.

I just want to make a note here: I normally do not go into
other men's hotel rooms. ~~It's not a good thing for this
whole minister gig I have going on.~~

An Unexpected Identity

Craig saw me coming and opened the door and invited
me in. We stood in front of the window and talked where
Larry could see us. He was eager to hear about the night
before. I not only shared all of that with him, but also
showed him the photos of my siblings. He was so
touched. All along as I shared my story I had also
passionately shared my faith. I told him about the hand of
God on my life. I spoke of how He had a plan for my life
that was yet unfolding. I told him about Jesus changing
my life even as a child, and how He would do this for
anyone, not just me! I shared about how He had given me
strength for the journey, and brought all of this together.
He was taking it in.

I asked him how his radio show went. He said it went
terrific. I asked a bit more about his work and he said,
"Well, actually, I'm an author. In fact, I'd love to give

you a copy of my latest book, the one I was here to do the show about yesterday. Would you read it?"

I said that I'd love to read it.

He went over to a box by his suitcase, pulled out one of the books and gave it to me. The book was called, *The Pro-Choice Victory Handbook: Strategies for Keeping Your Abortion Rights.*

I flipped the book over to read the bio on the back.

Craig was Craig Chilton, President of the Pro-Choice Action Network.

No. I. Am. Not. Kidding.

And there I was in his hotel room!

On one hand, I couldn't believe it. My thought was, "God, you are soooo hilarious to stick me in this guy's hotel room!" But on the other hand, it was not such a surprise. Those who know me well or are more familiar with my ministry know that God gives me crazy divine appointments on a regular basis. I believe one reason is because, I'm open. Willing to be interrupted. And perhaps most importantly—always try to communicate truth, with love. (Sometimes I fail, but love is the goal.)

You might wonder why a well-known author, speaker and activist was staying at Motel 6.

It boggles my mind, too.

All I can tell you is, it's true.

This really happened.

Larry can vouch for it.

I always thank God that when such out-of-the-ordinary things like this happen to me, most of the time there is a witness to verify that it really happened.

Craig and I had further conversation after his identity was revealed to me, about our differing views. We had a really nice talk. Not a debate, a conversation. After we were finished talking for a while, I asked if he'd come outside and meet Larry since he hadn't had the opportunity yet to do so. He was pleased to, and walked outside with me. Larry got out of the car and the three of us stood in the parking lot talking.

As we prepared to say goodbye, he said, "Deanna, can I just tell you this is perhaps the nicest conversation I've ever had with anyone on the other side?" He told me he had actually had chairs thrown at him by pro-lifers. He told me he was screamed at on a regular basis. I expressed my sadness about that. He said, "It's a great thing to have an open, friendly conversation like this, and I loved your story."

By the way, I did read his entire book on my way back home from Richmond. Did I agree with the book? No. My views are unchanged, however I believe it's important to do what I say I'm going to do. Second, I don't limit myself to reading things I agree with all the time. If my beliefs and values aren't strong enough to stand when being exposed to views other than my own, how powerful are they, really?

It's important that we keep open dialogue and seek understanding, even with those we don't agree with on principles.

Thank Yous are Always in Style

Before we headed to breakfast, I asked Larry to swing by a flower shop.

We got some roses and headed to the Woody Funeral Home.

I went in and asked for the assistant who had helped me. She was stunned to see me there, just two days after we spoke. I said, "You gave me my mother's name two days ago. I'm eternally grateful and just wanted to say thank you."

She said, "Honey, I told you—I was just doing my job."

I shared with her that doing one's job faithfully changes peoples' lives even when we don't always realize the impact. I gave her the flowers and asked if I could meet her boss. I expressed my thanks to him for the great job she was doing and told him she changed my life. He wanted to hear my story. So I told him everything you've just read. ~~As concisely as possible. My family was so hungry~~. After sharing it he said, "This is just... amazing! It's so nice to have an opportunity to help people who are alive!"

Three Divine Appointments are a Charm

We needed to pick up something at the motel room that we had forgotten so we swung back there on our way to breakfast at Aunt Sarah's Pancake House. I'm so glad we did! The forgotten item was also a divine moment, because as we came into the room the phone was ringing. Judy called and asked what our plans were.

We told her we were headed to the pancake house and she said, "I'll meet you there!" I had no idea how this would be possible since I thought she had to work and wondered what in the world was going on. Shortly thereafter she and Tom arrived at the restaurant and she informed us that she gathered with her coworkers that morning and told them the events of the night before.

I was shocked. We hadn't even talked about whether she was going to tell people or not tell them. I've learned that it's not uncommon for an adoptee's first mother to keep them a secret even after reunion. I was prepared for that possibility.

Judy told her coworkers that she had only told them about two of her children prior to this. She shared that I had come back into her life the night before, and that I would be in town the rest of the week. She made arrangements to take the week off to be with us. Her coworkers were absolutely thrilled and even begged to meet us. Judy arranged for us to meet a group of them while we were in town. In fact, she made plans for us to meet with all of her closest friends while we were there and introduce us.

It was one of the best weeks of my life.

When I look back, I would actually describe the week as magical.

Better than Disney.

We spent time together, talking, sharing meals, and for me it was a time of learning about my brother and sister.

We drove by the house where she grew up, at Tom's suggestion.

Tom pointed out things all the time that he thought I might care about. He's a person who gives attention to detail, with a heart for others as big as all outdoors. He would point out things around town that were meaningful to Judy—things he thought might interest me. Since I hadn't met them yet, he would describe things about my brother and sister. Tom would take note of what I ordered in a restaurant and say things like, "That's exactly what your sister would order!"

He seemed to be as excited about me meeting her as I was! He kept saying, "You have so much in common, you're just going to be amazed..." He was right.

Sibling Revelation

Judy called my siblings the day after our reunion to tell them of what took place. They had learned of me years prior.

My sister was shocked and a bit afraid to meet me. She had recently married and moved to Alaska with her husband, who was in the military. She felt overwhelmed with so much happening at once. Living far away, she didn't feel as much a part of things. Reunion even in the best of circumstances gets rocky at times, and my sister and I had a major adjustment period. Over time we would bond. We do have so much in common. Although she did not grow up in a Christian home, she too turned to God early in life. She has served and still continues to serve in missions. We always have a time of prayer together before we conclude any phone call, at her invitation.

My brother was thrilled from the get-go, and couldn't wait to meet.

On the day he learned I had found them, he went out to the Hallmark store, trying to find a card that would reflect his feelings. He came home without a card, sat down and started to create one at his computer. ~~Unfortunately for him, they don't sell, "Your sister found you years after being turned away by your mother after a botched confidential intermediary situation" cards. Nope, they don't sell those. What the heck is wrong with you, Hallmark?~~

I received his specially designed card in the mail a few days later. With tears streaming down my face, I read his words:

> *Deanna,*
>
> *Took you long enough to find me, didn't it?*
>
> *I love you,*
>
> *Your brother*

I met my brother a few weeks after this. My sister also flew from Alaska to meet me at our home in Ohio and spent the weekend with us.

We learned about many similarities as time unfolded. One day Tom remarked that he has a hard time distinguishing whether it is my sister or me talking! My brother and sister are also naturally musically gifted. (Surprise, surprise!)

The Great Alaskan Adventure

Reunion felt overwhelming at first when we realized how much catching up we had to do. And ultimately, we grasped we never would, no matter how hard we tried. I discovered it was possible to have a lot of great times together, but making up for lost time is something that never happens in the truest sense. That's not to say we didn't try. Particularly in the beginning, we tried intensely.

Judy wanted us to have more time together and things were a challenge with my sister living in Alaska. She arranged a trip for all of us to go to Alaska and spend eight days at my sister's home and also enjoy Denali.

It was a memorable trip, one none of us will ever forget. In addition to Judy, Tom and my brother, an uncle and two cousins also came along on the trip. It was a blast. We sat in a jacuzzi together having talks until late at night and made up our own crazy songs and inside jokes. We panned for gold and fished for salmon and took long walks.

One night we dined at a place that had a piano bar. They encouraged me to play a few songs for everyone to sing along. I happily obliged. The rest of the family members decided (without Judy and Tom's approval) to sing, "Going to the Chapel" (and we're gonna get married).

We were laughing hysterically!

Judy and Tom? Not so much.

They weren't happy with us.

They still had no designs on marriage. In fact, they got downright peeved. We sat there and laughed and laughed while the two of them just got madder!

But the tide was about to turn... in a significant way.

Chapter 8—
And I Think to Myself,
What a Wonderful World

"When all the details fit in perfectly, something is probably wrong with the story."

— *Charles Baxter,* Burning Down the House

Tom called me in late 1996 with a total surprise.

"Mel, (he has always called me Mel, short for Melanie) I'm considering proposing to your mother. Under one condition."

"Okkkkkkkkkayyyyyy," I said in utter shock. Both of them had sworn that they would NEVER get married again.

"What's the condition?" I asked cautiously.

"You must perform the wedding ceremony!" he answered.

"Are you serious?" I said, laughing with delight. "Of course I will. It would be an honor." I was overjoyed. Not only did he want me to marry them, he wanted to have the wedding at our church. By this time, Larry and I were senior pastors of North Carroll Assembly of God, in Manchester, Maryland, a congregation we would lead for ten years.

The proposal occurred and the wedding was planned. The ceremony took place on February 1, 1997, at our church and the reception was at a local restaurant, Greenmount Station. Their family and friends would make the trek from Richmond and various places for the wedding. I was seven months pregnant with our daughter, Savanna Rose. Looking as if I was about ready to pop, I stood at the altar in a black maternity dress with a white collar, trying to be all official-preacher-looking while almost ready to deliver a baby.

In addition to performing the ceremony, my sister and I sang a duet, "The Wedding Song: There is Love" by Peter, Paul and Mary.

Everyone present at the wedding knew our story. There was a lot of crying, all happy tears.

I got through the ceremony, controlling my emotions—maintaining professionalism as much as possible, but didn't make it all the way until the end. When I said, "I now pronounce you husband and wife. You may kiss the bride," I began to cry.

Tom did kiss his bride but immediately after, he turned to the family and friends gathered and announced, "And now, I've just gotta kiss the preacher!" With that, he planted a kissed my cheek, the three of us standing in a tearful group hug.

Many more tears. Happy tears.

~~It was more like a Kleenex moment than a Kodak moment.~~

My brother's wedding was another unforgettable occasion. He asked me to be in the wedding party while Larry performed the ceremony. He gave me an engraved bracelet with my name and the date on it as a special gift. I keep it in my jewelry box because I don't want anything to happen to it.

We have enjoyed special times over the past twenty years, moments that are tucked away in my heart now.

Perfect World?

By now you may be reading our story thinking, "How much more perfect could this be?"

Friends have sat across the table from me at coffee shops while I've shared this and practically sobbed their eyeballs out thinking it's the most amazing fairytale they've ever heard.

Not quite.

There were many ups and downs over the last twenty years. I've learned that reunion is a rollercoaster ride even in the very best case scenarios. Mine is no exception.

For instance, the first time my adoptive mom heard me call Judy, "Mom," was a lihhhhttle bit of a problem. ~~It was worse than Watergate.~~ It came out naturally, at a birthday party for one of my kids, and I recall her saying it was "like a knife to her heart." We had a little ~~okay, a big~~ scene. That was one of the first times I can remember standing up for myself. I shared how I was feeling in the moment, rather than suppressing it.

There have been meltdowns, with multiple family members on both sides, over time.

Perhaps the question that is most difficult for me—more than any other, is the one I am asked most, "How is your [adoptive] mother doing with all of this?"

Why does this question bother me so much? Because people never ask, "How are YOU doing with all this?" I am the one who was actually adopted.

Many adoptees I've talked to share the same exact experience. Everyone asks about their adoptive mom but no one ever thinks to ask about them. Everybody in the world must have gotten the memo to ask about adoptive moms. It's rather strange that almost no one inquires about how the person who is actually adopted feels.

My Job Description

For the most part, my adoptee job description was unwritten or unspoken, but there were times when some individuals shared my apparent job description. An aunt once scolded me, saying, "Your job is to bring your mother happiness!" It appeared that some believed my mother had needs and desires I was sent by God to fulfill. Evidently I was failing at a job I never signed up for.

Because of comments like this, as well as things sensed but unspoken, I felt pressured at times. It is a tremendous weight to be responsible for the happiness of another person, and furthermore, it is not a God-given assignment, therefore it causes such strain.

Adoptive parents sometimes have unrealistic expectations for a child to fill a void in their lives, or bring healing— particularly those who cannot conceive or bear children. Even when an infertile couple adopts, they still grieve the infertility, as well they should. Infertility is a traumatic ordeal and one I have great compassion for, as any painful human experience. But an adoptee shouldn't pay the price for this loss. There's a difference between possession and love. I do understand why a couple paying upwards of $50,000 in many cases for an infant, would want exclusive rights to him or her. But the reality is that anytime you try to own or possess a human being, rather than love him or her, there's bound to be trouble.

On this issue, Christian therapist Bonnie Zello Martin, Med, CACS, LCPC shares, "It is also often the case that adoption meets a significant need in those who seek to adopt. This places a great responsibility on the adoptee. Any expression of trauma, loss or grief, or identity exploration by adopted children can be misinterpreted as rejection of the adopted parent(s). When this happens, the result is usually an inappropriate role reversal in the parent/child relationship. The child is responsible for the parent's unmet needs instead of vice versa. Such a child will either comply with the rules of engagement—suffering tremendous anxiety, or the child will refuse the role reversal and act out, appearing as angry/rebellious/ungrateful."

I'm Walking on ~~Sunshine~~ Eggshells

Was my adoption about finding a home for me? Or was it about finding a child for a needy couple?

Until I was in my forties, I never dared to ask these questions out loud.

When I did have the courage to ask them, it was painful, yet freeing.

Sadly, almost every week there are adoptees who write to me privately to tell me they liked one of my posts and wanted to click "like" on Facebook, or make a comment, but could not bring themselves to do it. The reason was because if someone in their family noticed they had done so, it would bring devastating repercussions in their relationship. There's something wrong when grown men and women fear that clicking "like" on an article will cause devastation in their family. Unfortunately, I understand this dilemma. My thought in sharing my feelings for most of my life was, "I've already lost so much, and if by speaking my feelings out loud I will lose even more, it would be best just to suppress myself."

I believe one reason that people can be so touchy when it comes to the subject of adoption is because there is often so much pain present among all of the parties. The natural parent, adoptive parents, and adoptee have all experienced tremendous losses despite their gains.

Searching and Betrayal

Some of my adoptive family members felt that my search was a betrayal. I quickly found out that I was not alone in facing that response. I discovered that when adoptees open up concerning their desire to learn more about their natural family or search for them, it is often viewed by their adoptive family, and even others who may have no connection to adoption, as a betrayal.

Adoptees are often considered disloyal if we simply express our desire for knowledge or reunion. Pursuing my natural family was not about dishonoring anyone, but instead it was about honoring two families. I believe an adoptive family will only be strengthened by honoring the natural family of their adopted family member.

Two Families, Neither Erased

I am fascinated by this quote from the book *Without a Map*, written by Meredith Hall:

Women carry fetal cells from all the babies they have carried. Crossing the defensive boundaries of our immune system and mixing with our own cells, the fetal cells circulate in the mother's bloodstream for decades after each birth. The body does not tolerate foreign cells, which trigger illness and rejection. But a mother's body incorporates into her own the cells of her children as if they recognize each other. This fantastic melding of two selves, mother and child is called microchimerism... the mother's cells are also carried in the child. During gestation, maternal cells slip through the barriers of defense and join her child's cells as they pulse through his veins... of course the implications are stunning. Mother and child do not fully separate at birth. We do not lose each other at that moment of severance.

Every child who is ever born in this world has a natural mother and father. Sometimes they take responsibility and are involved in their child's life. Other times not. This doesn't mean they cease to exist.

My natural family was not erased.

Even though my OBC was sealed.

Even though my adoptive parents moved us 147 miles away from the city where they adopted me.

Even though we didn't know each other's new names. (My natural mother married and changed hers. My adoptive parents changed mine.)

We were still connected even before reunion, and always will be.

I'm not sure there's any more challenging place to be than connected and disconnected at the same time.

I wanted desperately (and still want) everyone to be understanding and accepting of my need to connect with both families. To stop jockeying for position and just love. Reunion can be the ultimate familial tug-of-war with the adoptee at the center, drowning in the mud.

Recently I received a letter from an adoptee who wrote, "You seem like such a well-adjusted adoptee in reunion... please show me how to have this kind of healthy reunion."

My reunion contained magical moments, for sure.

There have also been really painful ones.

I'm not a reunion expert, by far. I'm just a fellow traveler. I have gone through times of difficulty, and it's God's grace and community that cover so much and carry me through the challenges.

Several years ago, in what has become one of the greatest blessings of my life, I connected with the adoptee community and become an active part; I gained some of the most wonderful friendships of my life and received a different kind of support than I ever experienced previously.

Little did I realize how much more I would need grace to increase, twenty years after reunion. I would need God's help like never before, and the support of the community to survive the blow that was coming.

Chapter 9—
Wanted: Two Words

"Secrets, silent, stony sit in the dark palaces of both our hearts: secrets weary of their tyranny: tyrants willing to be dethroned."

— *James Joyce*

Even though I was in active relationship with the maternal side of my family, I learned quickly that reunion doesn't magically solve everything. Something inside me did settle down to a degree once I met Judy and my siblings. Yet, reuniting with my natural maternal family did not change the complexity I faced in the way I fit in or relate to both families.

I have been told, "You aren't adopted... you *were* adopted. That is past. Now, you just need to leave the past behind and move on."

The signing of a paper doesn't mean my natural family doesn't exist. It just means somebody wrote on a piece of paper.

I will always be adopted, as much as some would like to believe it all changed the moment a few papers were signed. My adoptive family will always be my family. My natural family will always be my family. I have two families.

"Do you know your real mother?" I have been asked countless times.

"Actually, all of my family members are real," I respond.

None of them are extra-terrestrial beings, although I have sometimes felt like one.

Why Didn't I Speak Up?

Some people are surprised I had any post-adoption struggles at all or felt the need to connect with the adoptee community, because for so long, I never spoke of my challenges publicly.

I have learned this is common for adoptees.

First of all, when you're young, you don't even know what to call it. Even a youngster who is gifted in communication skills is hard-pressed to define it. I could always express myself, yet as a child I would not have

been comfortable enough to tell my parents what I was
really feeling.

Second, the majority of the world has no understanding
where adult adoptees are coming from, particularly in the
Christian world. I say this not to bash Christians. (I am
one!) I share this to try to bring understanding.

When Christian adoptees gather enough courage to
express themselves, they often encounter a quick rebuttal
about Moses being adopted, Jesus being adopted, and
their identity being in Christ.

"Your real parents are the ones who changed your
diapers!" people say profusely. "We're all adopted in
Christ...what's the big deal?"

"Just accept that you're a child of the King!"

You hear James 1:27 quoted again and again.

You are admonished about everything from being
grateful you weren't an abortion, to hearing about other
adoptees who are perfectly happy with no desire to
search. "My neighbor has two adopted kids and they are
as happy as can be! What's wrong with you? Did your
adoption just not work out?"

People don't seem to grasp the idea that you can deeply
love your adoptive family, yet not love everything that
happened to you.

You are expected to express no feelings other than elation
about your relinquishment and adoption. All this results
in learning to be quiet unless you want to hurt more.

Many of my friends in the adoptee community have shared the important truth that just because we express pain or a desire for reform in adoption does not mean we do not love our adoptive families. But so often, when we raise questions, discuss our feelings, decide to search, or mention a desire for reform in the institution of adoption, it is labeled a betrayal.

Regarding my adoption, I've often been encouraged by Christians to delight in the fact I am "chosen"… "different"… and "special."

A person may dream of standing out from the crowd because of our art work, sportsmanship or a plethora of other good things. But nobody wants to stand out and be part of the 2% of people in the world whose mothers relinquished them. It's vastly different than standing out because you're the valedictorian of your class, or because you've got an amazing voice.

Most of us want to stand out from the crowd for the happy things in life.

Being permanently separated from your biological parents, losing your entire extended first family, and being given to strangers isn't one of the ways in which anyone dreams of being different. And to be adopted, that has to happen first. In my personal experience, most people act as if the loss never happened. If they do acknowledge that the loss occurred, they usually follow up by telling me to praise God for it.

I have discovered that my experience is not rare. Christian therapist Bonnie Zello Martin, MEd, CACS, LCPC shares, "There is a little known psychological term called 'spiritual bypass.' Spiritual bypass is when we engage in religious beliefs and activities in order to avoid or cover up uncomfortable emotions, unmet needs, deep wounds, or hidden fears. In the church, adoption is most often viewed as a righteous, selfless act of rescue, or a ministry or higher calling. The glorification of the act of adopting unfortunately results in 'bypassing' the fact that separation from biological parents, at any stage of development, is traumatic."

These are a few reasons why I never spoke about this publicly for most of my life. As an adoptee, you have already lost one family and the thing that scares you more than anything is losing another.

Only my husband, a few close friends, and two counselors knew of the issues I struggled with. Who wants to get a verbal pelting if you speak up about what is your actual life experience? Perhaps there is nothing more frustrating than people who haven't lived something all their lives telling people who HAVE lived it since birth, how they should feel about it, not to mention what the laws should be about it.

One Missing Part Still Crying Out

At peace with the knowledge and the relationship with my maternal family, there was still part of me missing.

My natural father.

Twenty years of reunion on my maternal side had now passed without knowing anything about my father.

Judy had made it clear; he wasn't a subject up for discussion. It was hard for me to mount up the courage to go there again. After everything I went through to gain not only knowledge of, but an active relationship with her and my siblings as well as Tom, I didn't want to ruin it.

My sister had inquired over the years, asking about him.

She said she believed that it was very important for me to know the truth.

Yet Judy was a vault—with the information of my past sealed up tight. That's an important factor in this—my father's identity is MY past too.

I began to pray about it over the years and think about how to approach the subject of obtaining the knowledge of who my father is, or was, in a way that would not harm mine and Judy's relationship.

Time is Tickin' Away

The years were going by and I realized my natural father, if still alive, was not getting any younger. Time was running out to find him. I had kept the peace with Judy and still had not been kicked out of the kitchen. Yet my heart longed to know... Who is my father? What does he look like? Apparently I favor him a lot, this "Greek God."

I try and try to imagine what he looks like. What his voice sounds like. I assumed the searching out faces in public places would leave when I reunited with Judy. But it doesn't. I still stare into men's faces everywhere, especially ones who are elderly Greek men, focusing in on their unique features, wondering if they are my father. I try to look away nonchalantly, if they notice I am staring at them.

There is an older Greek gentleman who plays the guitar at the Acropolis, our favorite Greek restaurant in Tampa. My son Dustin thinks he's a poor guitarist. (Dustin is a great guitarist.) But when he brings this up I always say, "Shush! I love this man!" I always envision... maybe he is really my natural father, uprooted and replanted from Richmond, Virginia to Tampa, Florida. It's possible, right? He's Greek. He's a musician. And, he's old.

Dustin thinks he should be disqualified simply because he's not a good musician.

All my children are good musicians.

They couldn't be this man's grandchildren, I think with a smile.

So my family took me there on Mother's Day to eat and sure enough he was playing the guitar that day, and I had all the same thoughts. Because I just don't know.

I fantasize that my father is the guitar player at the Acropolis.

I have nightmares that my father is a serial killer.

You do this when you have no idea who your natural father is.

You watch a TV show and see a man and think, "Maybe that's my father."

You just want it to stop.

You want it to settle down inside you.

You just want the truth.

Going to a concert or ballgame needs to be about the concert and the ballgame, not studying faces of strangers to see if they have your nose.

None of this means that I don't love my adoptive father.

It's of note that you can still love your adoptive father but hate the fact that you have no idea who your natural father is.

My Plan B: DNA

Through my involvement in the adoptee community I became aware of DNA testing as a relatively new means of finding one's biological family. Several of my adoptee friends had found natural parents through this means and a few are currently in process. Some had suggested this technology as a means of finding my father.

Many who have never heard of this before have said to me, "Why would you search through criminal databases to find your father? What if he has never committed a crime?"

These DNA databases have nothing to do with criminals. Some people's only exposure to talk of DNA is through hearing about crimes or court cases, so I do understand this question. Actually DNA technology goes beyond that and is available for different purposes. One of the reasons you can do DNA today is genealogy or finding lost family.

There are several companies that can be utilized for this purpose—three of them being FamilyTreeDNA, Ancestry, and 23andMe. People have also assumed it must be a tremendous expense. Actually they are very affordable.

I was grateful for this option but hoped I wouldn't have to use it.

I considered it an act of respect to ask Judy once more, as well. If I pursued my father through DNA and found him, I didn't plan on hiding it. I would never flaunt the discovery of him to Judy as I knew her discomfort with the subject of him. But I also considered that someone else might tell her if I reunited with him, and it would come as a shock. I didn't want to blindside her or hurt her in any way by living a secret.

The Letter

I decided to write Judy a letter since I express myself best in writing. I don't always recommend people sending letters because writing doesn't communicate true tone and intent every time. Unless one is a really good writer, handling things by e-mail and such can be a disaster. People in my life tell me it's most meaningful to them when they receive my communications in writing. They say my heart shines through more clearly when I write than when I speak. I wanted to ask Judy in the most effective way possible, which is why I settled on this way of doing it. I still don't regret it.

The first part of the letter was chit-chat that has no bearing here, things about both of our hobbies and upcoming family events. The heart of it, about my original father said the following:

> *Judy,*
>
> *Finding you years ago brought a level of healing that I needed desperately. I thank you for accepting and including me and giving me the gift of not only you and Tom, but my brother and sister as well. I love them both, but in particular the relationship I have with my sister is an amazing treasure. I know as the years grow on we will achieve her dream of becoming like you and your sister, maybe beyond, who knows?*
>
> *One missing puzzle piece in my life still remains, that of my father. I know nothing about him. Except the fact that he is Greek. And you told me I look like him. I would like to know more, anything you can tell me. I know it's not a pleasant subject for you and a chapter of your life that is closed, but for me it is still an open chapter that I wonder about a lot and have never been able to be at peace about.*
>
> *I told you the first night we were reunited that I did not come to make your life difficult or make demands on you. And I hope I have lived up to that for these twenty years. I still desire to cause no harm, I simply want to know the entirety of my heritage, where and who I come from. Can we*

open up a conversation about me learning my father's name and more about him, together?

I miss you lots and hope to talk to you soon.

Love you,

~Deanna

I e-mailed the letter on February 26, 2013.

Little did I know, it would unleash a firestorm.

Chapter 10 — Losing Her for the Third Time

"Truth and roses have thorns about them."

— *Henry David Thoreau*

Roses and I have a long-standing relationship. When my parents adopted me and brought me to my Grandma Lewis for the first time, she called me "Rosebud." It stuck. Nobody else ever called me that, but she did, all the time. She also had many rose bushes in her yard and they flourished under her care.

This is why we named our daughter Savanna Rose. I wanted a part of my story and my grandmother's impact on my life to live on in my daughter's name even when I pass on some day. I know my grandmother will always impact Savanna's life simply because it is reflected in the way I've raised her, having been influenced by such an amazing woman of God.

When we named Savanna Rose, we spelled her name as such with no "h" at the end because we wanted half of her first name to be identical to mine, ending in "anna."

We chose her first name because we liked it and it sort of mirrored mine without being identical but little did I know that, to me it would come to mean even more in the future. Ten years after her birth, God would open up a door for me to preach in East Africa, not once but many times. I was invited by Dr. Bill and Barbara Kuert, strangers to me when I was first invited to come to be the keynote speaker for the national women's conference for the Kenya Assemblies of God. Bill and Barb have since become some of my dearest friends. The first message that I ever preached in East Africa was about women in the Bible who were broken, shamed, and sexually abused. God spoke to me to have a healing service for those who were victims. The floodgates of heaven were open that night in East Africa.

I would go on to have the privilege of ministering to thousands of women there over the coming years on many subsequent preaching trips. "Savanna" spelled as such with no "h" is the name of the plain in East Africa, the Savanna—a part of the world I long for all the time. Not a day goes by when I don't think of and pray for East Africa and the beautiful people I now consider family.

I love how God orders things when we seek Him. He beautifully writes the story. People say I'm a gifted storyteller. Truthfully, God writes the story, and guides me in how to best share it. When I write, I feel His presence.

I've come to realize just how important names are.

A name is so important, it can lead you home.

So, Savanna Rose is my daughter's name—rich with meaning and even greater significance years later than the day she was born.

People say, "Life isn't a bed of roses..."

Wanna make a bet?

It is. I know this for sure. I've laid in a bed of roses before.

Not just the ones that are strewn around the room on a romantic getaway.

Rosebud Lays in the Rose Bush

When I was a kid I was friends with a kid named Clayton Radcliffe, called Clay Joe by his grandmother, who cared for him a lot of the time. She lived on the other street that was adjacent to North Dakota Avenue, which was Lincoln Avenue.

Clayton and I rode bikes together, played hide-and-seek, and had all kinds of good fun. Occasionally we got into a spat, like all kids do. Clayton was actually a really good kid, but one day I ticked him off about something and he pushed me into a bed of rose bushes. I ended up falling off balance and lying right on top of it. The thorns pressed into my upper arms and the back of my calves, the most exposed areas.

Oh, the pain!

Managing to stand up was quite the feat as with every move, more thorns dug into other areas of my body. I got up and went to clean up and vaguely remember something about making a mud pie the next day, taking vengeance into my own hands. ~~Don't be fooled. I am not a Pentecostal Mother Teresa even though my mother-in-law thinks I am.~~

Clayton was a good sport. We patched things up and were right back to riding bikes and catching lightning bugs.

Roses are still my favorite flower, not just because Grandma Lewis called me "Rosebud," but because to me, by their very form, they speak of the reality of life.

Real life is beautiful but not void of painful points.

Life is very much a bed of roses.

A New Bed of Roses for Rosebud

Tuesday went by. Nothing.

Wednesday went by. Nothing.

Then Thursday came.

February 28, 2013.

I believed the best for what was to come. Just like I had believed in 1990 that Judy would agree to the confidential intermediary, my heart leaned toward believing she was going to say yes to me now. I believed she would think about it, and ultimately e-mail me his name.

Part of my reasoning behind sending the e-mail was also because I thought it might be easier for her just to type the name rather than actually talk about it. I really thought in my heart she was going to type the name and click send.

Why did I believe this?

I had faith for it. And twenty years of good adoptee behavior.

Did it count for something?

My husband said it didn't.

He begged me to not get my hopes up. He was so afraid I was going to get hurt again.

Larry has always had the gift of discernment, but this time I was really praying he was wrong.

Two Words

Keep in mind, this was all I was asking for: his name.

Two words.

I wasn't asking her to tell me the circumstances of my conception.

I wasn't asking her to go back and re-live the whole thing.

I wasn't asking her for intimate details.

I wasn't asking her to face my father, talk to my father, or see my father.

I wasn't asking her to have anything to do with my father ever again.

I was asking for two words.

A man's first and last names.

I would handle everything from there, and ask nothing else of her.

While I am not the owner of my mother's personal information, I am the rightful owner of mine. The name of my father is my personal information as well. So technically, we are co-owners of his identity.

Unfortunately, everything isn't decided on a technicality.

The Phone Call that Changed Everything

Our home phone rang and Larry picked it up. He called to me that Judy was on the phone.

We chit-chatted for about ten minutes about Savanna Rose's Sweet Sixteen party coming up in April. I was in the process of planting a bunch of rose bushes in the backyard—just for the party, as my daughter had requested.

No. I. Am. Not. Kidding.

Pink roses, yellow roses, red roses, even purplish roses.

Pinterest shows no easy way to do this... you just have to get out there and dig a bunch of deep holes and start planting them. ~~In the end, only one of those blasted bushes has turned out to look like my grandmother's.~~

Let's Get this Paternity Party Started... (Or Not.)

Then I said, "Well, I guess you got my email."

She said, "Yes, I did, and I thought it deserved a phone call, for something like this." Quickly getting to the point she said, "I'm sorry, Deanna. I'm just not going to go there. I'm not going to give you his name."

"Okaaaaaaaaaaaaaaay," I said. "So, that's it? You're just not going to tell me who my father is?"

"No, I'm not," she curtly said.

Tentatively I said, "Well, the years are going by, and I'm running out of time. How long do I have to wait for his name?"

She went on to say that she was never going to tell me. Ever.

I said, "Do you believe that human beings have a right to know who their mother and father are?"

"I don't know about all that, but I'm saying in this case, in your case, I am not going to tell you who he is," she answered. "No one currently alive knows who your father is. The only two people who did know are now dead. This is a secret that will go with me to my grave one day."

I pushed back, albeit gently, and let her know I didn't agree with the decision, that I had a right to know my father's name.

"No, you don't," she said. "It's settled. There's no one to ask about this. There is no one besides me who knows, not even Tom. Not my sister. Not your sister. No one. So you don't even need to ask anyone. You need to let this go. Be at peace. You're beautiful, Deanna. You're smart. You've raised an amazing family. You're a success. Be happy with all that, and just go on. Move on with life."

She repeated this last part three times.

It was her sticking point.

All that mattered was that I've turned out well, and now I needed to just move on and forget everything else, which was now—according to her, a moot point.

But my father is not a moot point, any more than she is a moot point. I come from them. Both of them.

Now I am a grown woman, wanting to know the truth. I want to know the basic information of who both of my natural parents are, and in response I am being treated as a perpetual child.

Perhaps most frustrating was that my personal information was not lost.

It was not unknown, to everyone.

Judy knew exactly what I was asking for.

She could solve it in two seconds.

Yet she outright refused to give me what she readily admitted she had!

She wanted to know why I couldn't just let it go and be happy. "Is this because you're connected with the adoptee community?"

I explained that this wasn't the case at all. Certainly the adoptee community has provided a place of understanding for me. But having the truth of my earthly identity concealed from me has been a challenge. I don't want to let it go when it comes to my father for the same reason I couldn't just let it go with her.

I had asked about my father before. But I hadn't wanted to lose Judy, and I tried my best to "be good" and not push. I told her I didn't have the courage.

"Courage?" She said, incredulous. "I don't believe that for one minute! There's no way the person who knocked on my door unannounced twenty years ago did not have the courage! I don't buy it... not for a second! If there's one thing you have, Deanna, it's courage."

"No, no, that's not true," I explained. "I don't always have courage every moment. There are times I'm afraid. Times I'm very afraid, and in many instances, I have to press beyond my fear into faith. Sometimes it takes me longer to step out. This is one of those times. It's taken everything in me to gather the courage to ask you again."

I explained that I had been calculating the risk.

I had more to lose now. An active twenty-year relationship with her, with my siblings, with Tom. I was still holding back so many of my desires so as to not hurt others. The years going by were prodding me to go there again, to a place I was so afraid of, before it was too late.

She couldn't accept it, no matter my explanation, and said it was over, end of discussion, and I needed to just be happy with what I had and move on.

The Sentence that Blew Up my World

"Well, I really wanted to be respectful about this and ask you again before I explore other options," I said.

"I'm not sure what you mean by that," she haltingly said. "There are no other options. I'm the only one who knows his name, so there's nothing left to do."

I took a deep breath.

"Well, actually it's not settled with me," I said quietly. "I am considering DNA testing as the next step, but really hoping I don't have to do that. I wanted to do the right thing and ask you again, first."

And then...

All. Hell. Unleashed.

The entire story changed.

Again.

For the third time.

Everything was entirely different from what she told me the night we reunited.

And completely different from what she told the adoption agency, and what I had received in my non-identifying information.

How many times could my personal history change?

"I never told the adoption agency the truth, Deanna. And I didn't tell you the truth either. I couldn't."

"Well, tell me the truth now," I said.

"No. I'm just not willing to go there."

Why? Why? Why?

Even if he is what society would term "the worst of the worst," I want to know.

If he is a terrorist being held at Guantanamo Bay, I want to know.

If he is Jimmy Hoffa, I want to know. ~~That's right. It can't be Jimmy Hoffa. Jimmy was born in 1913.~~

~~If he is the person ultimately responsible for taking Twinkies away from the American people, I want to know.~~

I gently asked, "So, is he really Greek? Am I really Greek?"

I had a strong feeling the Greek part was still the truth, since back in 2009 I was diagnosed with a medical condition that primarily affects Greeks and Italians. (And to my knowledge, my mother is neither.)

"Yes," she said. "He is part Greek."

Suddenly she offered up that she had also lied about his age, to the agency, and to me.

Instead of him being 29, as she and the agency had told me all along, she now suddenly changed his age to 33 at the time of my birth.

Quickly I realized if she was telling the truth with this brand new story, he would be 80 now.

~~Well truthfully, it wasn't quickly... I totally stink at math, even basic math. So I pulled up my calculator on the screen and added 33 and 47.~~

I said, "Okay, so according to what you're saying now, he would be 80-years-old at this time. Perhaps he is dead, or if he is not, he is elderly. What do you fear about me knowing his name now, all these years later? The main thing I want is a name and a photo, even if he has passed away or I am not able to find him."

"He's not worthy of being found!" she angrily snapped.

"Remember, you said you weren't worthy of being found," I countered.

"He's a different kind of not-worthy-to-be-found!" she shot back.

"I'm so sorry this is so painful for you," I said. "I don't want to cause you pain. I am hoping you know that would never be my intention, based on knowing my character the last twenty years. I just want to know my father's name. That's all I want to know. It's all I've ever asked you for."

She got angrier and more insistent that I would never know his name and needed to give up.

I decided to try a different line of questioning.

"How long did you date my father?"

"We never dated!" she snapped back.

I was perplexed by this new revelation as well, since on our first night of reunion I was told that they did date, and then she became pregnant with me and he did not support her. For the past twenty years, Larry had jokingly quipped to people, "Despite what her natural father says, I know my wife definitely exists—I pay her bills!" This joke came from all the years of believing what Judy told Larry and me on the night we were reunited.

Hearing this new information, I responded with, "Okay then, you are saying you never dated him or asked him for support. Does this mean you had no prior relationship with my father? Was he a stranger? What exactly does this mean? Are you saying you were raped?"

"Basically."

"What does 'basically' mean?" I asked.

She didn't answer.

Carefully measuring my words, I said, "I understand why that would be absolutely devastating. If this is the case, I feel terrible about the fact that you went through this. I just want to clarify what you mean by *basically*. What does 'basically' mean?"

Silence.

Moments later she would repeat once more that she was "basically raped," but never clarify what this meant.

"Okay… I'm not accusing you of being untruthful. I just have questions in light of this new information. Like… how does referring to my father as your 'Greek God' fit in with him being a rapist?"

"I don't know…" she said. "I just said it. I don't know why I said it. I can't explain it."

She would go on to say that she referred to him as a Greek God because, "You came to the door and were so beautiful and I just blurted it out without thinking."

Later in the conversation and by letter she would also tell me she couldn't bring herself to tell me I was conceived from rape because of "the lovely pink suit and pink bow that I was wearing" when I came to her door in 1993.

I have asked myself again and again what the "loveliness" of my apparel could possibly have to do with a reluctance or refusal to tell me the truth.

The conversation never got any clearer and continued to go around with no resolution.

The more she talked, the more confused I became.

She underscored that her original plan was to conceal my father's identity from everyone in her life. The new story she revealed to me that night was that she had no intention of telling her mother my father's identity. She lied to the adoption agency—blaming the pregnancy on a man she worked with at the drug store. She claimed that the social worker who was handling my adoption shared with her mother that the man she named as my father worked with her at the drugstore. Armed with this new information, her mother marched down to the drugstore to confront the man. "How dare you get my daughter pregnant!" she said.

He responded, "I have no idea what you're talking about. I've never been with your daughter!"

Judy's mother could tell the man at the drugstore was telling the truth. She confronted her, saying she had spoken to the man at the drug store and he had denied all involvement. She demanded to know who my father was and Judy told her the truth, with the caveat that she never reveal the information to anyone, including her father. According to Judy, her mother agreed to it and went to her grave with the secret of my father's identity.

"Why are you protecting him? Why are you so insistent on keeping my father's identity a secret?" I asked.

"He's not your father! He's not *a* father! He's a monster!" she said. "And just to let you know, I'm sure you have a whole bunch of brothers and sisters. Because this is just who he is and what he does!"

"What do you mean?"

"He preys on young girls. He goes from girl to girl, and then moves on like nothing ever happened!"

"How do you know that?" I asked.

She answered that she kept up with him throughout the years, taking note of his ongoing inappropriate behavior towards women.

Does one normally "keep up with" a rapist, down through the years? I wrestle with this question. It's something I laid awake at night and wondered about, for many nights since.

I honestly don't know.

I wrestled with questions about the issue of her going back to talk to him about my conception. Do raped women normally go back to tell a rapist they are pregnant or ask them for any type of support? Why would anyone think a rapist might actually support them…with anything?

I also wonder why the confidential intermediary mentioned nothing about rape, twenty years earlier. I grappled at the time with understanding the reason for secondary rejection and pleaded with the CI to tell me why Judy had chosen to decline reunion. The CI was so kind, and understanding and kept reaffirming that it was because my mother felt there were failures in her own life that she could not face me with… that she felt "unworthy to be found." Why was nothing said about rape?

And what exactly did Judy tell the CI, if anything? What was her explanation at that point in time?

All of these questions were troubling for me.

"Do you feel better talking about this? Because I sure don't feel any better now!" she cried. "In fact, I was doing great! Tom and I were happy. Life was wonderful... and then THIS!"

Apparently, I had just ruined everything.

"Well, since you've asked, I do feel better hearing the truth, even if it is painful. While I am very sad about anything that hurt you, I want you to understand that whatever the truth is, it's not hearing it or processing it that devastates me. I can handle the truth. It is the unknown that hurts the most."

And then, a Verbal Holocaust

I was speaking with my mother, who I had been reunited with for twenty years, yet felt like I was talking to a person I had never met before.

She would go on to tell me that she was faking during the reunion, even up to two years into it… that she was just acting. "You can even ask Tom!" she said.

I couldn't even wrap my mind around this latest revelation.

I thought of us standing out by the car on the first night of reunion, and her crying and telling me she didn't want to let me go...

That was all... an act?

Twenty years had been... completely FAKE?

I felt like I had just been shot in the chest.

Repeatedly.

What was the truth of our relationship? Of our beginnings? Of our reunion? Suddenly she spilled out that none of this part of my life was what I thought it was.

It just felt like the room was spinning around me and would never stop. With every word that came out of her mouth, I felt myself crumbling inside.

In her typical roundabout way of telling me something yet not stating it outright, she indicated she was sorry I found her.

That moment may have been the worst in my life, and I'm sure one of the worst for her too. The pain that hung over the invisible phone line was palpable, with no relief in sight for either of us.

I still didn't believe her. At that moment, and even now, I believe she was glad we reunited... until I asked for my father's name.

Until.

Our relationship would always be fine on the surface... until I asked for the truth.

Truth was always the deal-breaker in our relationship.

Should I have been sorry for asking for something that's mine in the first place?

There has always been a tug-of-war between wanting to stay in her good graces and the desire for truth. I know I would have regretted not asking her for it while I still could, despite the searing pain it brought to both of us.

Turning to the Sisters

I clicked over to the private Facebook page of the Lost Daughters bloggers, my adoptee sisters who have been so supportive, providing invaluable insight on post-adoption issues. "Is anyone there?" I typed. "Judy is on the phone with me and all hell has just unleashed." Many of them quickly popped up online and began to hold me up and bring comfort. During the conversation, they posted constant words of affirmation:

"We are right here with you, Deanna..."

"You are not alone..."

"We are holding you close right now..."

"You do not face this moment alone..."

"You are loved..."

"We are here to help you walk through this..."

"We are holding you up..."

"You are going to make it through this!"

"You are a survivor..."

They would continue to hold me up with their words, late into the night and early into the morning as some of them stayed with me...

"You don't understand what it's like to be a birth mother," she said.

Granted, I don't. I know that I will never fully understand. But I try to.

Since Judy wouldn't open up over the years, I tried to learn all I could without her help. I've studied about that time period and what women went through back then, for hundreds—possibly thousands of hours. I have befriended many women in the first mother community. I have asked them questions and opened my heart to try to grasp it. I've read books about it and wept until I could weep no more, at what millions of girls and women suffered. But we can't have those kinds of conversations, because she is not open, at all.

I know there are injustices being committed now, but I am particularly grieved by what my mother's generation endured.

I seek to help, not to hurt.

I want to understand what it's like to be her.

Many people have asked me what she thinks of my writing about adoption. She told me she doesn't read my writing on the subject.

During our conversation she said the community was a "virus" and "something I needed to get away from as soon as possible."

These writings... they are "a sickness," she said.

"No," I retorted, "Actually what makes a person sick are secrets, lies, and denial! Not support groups and community, or writing!"

Okay.

~~That went over about as well as a Spanish restaurant running out of rice.~~

~~As effective as the guys from Duck Dynasty doing a commercial for Gillette Razors.~~

It was absolutely true but just threw more fuel on the fire. ~~Save me now, sweet Lord, baby Jesus.~~

New strategy:

Breathe in. Breathe out. Calm down.

I asked if I had been a blessing to her the past twenty years.

I asked if I had ever asked her for anything prior to this.

She said that I had not asked her for anything, and that I had been a blessing.

I let her know how bad the words were hurting.

How much I was aching in that moment.

Trying to grasp the latest revelation that our reunion was fake was like trying to stand in a hurricane as I struggled to finish our conversation that night.

"Please, Mom," my voice faltered… "Can you please just hear me and try to understand?"

"I don't care about your pain and quite frankly I don't want to hear about it!" she tersely said.

The entire time she spoke I kept thinking to myself, "This can't be real… this can't be happening…"

I tried so hard to keep my composure, to stay level-headed and kind.

She finished by quoting part of the "Serenity Prayer," telling me I needed to "accept that which I couldn't change."

The call ended with her curtly letting me know this was a closed subject.

And she said if I pursued DNA, we were done.

She said goodbye.

I had just lost her, for the third time.

I hung up the phone and fell over on my bed, wailing.

Chapter 11— The Aftermath (A.K.A. "Is Anyone There?")

"Give sorrow words; the grief that does not speak knits up the o-er wrought heart and bids it break."

— *William Shakespeare*

Larry and I had an explosive fight years ago because I never wanted to have a dog again. And he wanted one very badly.

I am crazzzzzzy about dogs. So it didn't make sense to him. The truth is, I was afraid of saying goodbye to a dog we didn't even have yet. Being that I feared goodbyes terribly, I felt it would be best if I never brought another dog into my world, that way I wouldn't have to say goodbye to it someday.

Larry won.

Now we have two dogs.

They were both tiny puppies when we got them. Maddie, an English Bulldog/Boxer mix, adjusted well to coming home with us and from the first night, went into her kennel at night to sleep and did just fine. Max, an American Bulldog, didn't do well. He cried and cried.

I never let our kids cry it out, and I wasn't about to let a puppy do that either. Max was so tiny when Larry brought him home, I could carry him around in the palm of one hand. I was instantly smitten. He would whimper if ever left alone, so I didn't leave him except to go to church services. I took him to the church office for work. If I was at home working, he sat right beside me, snuggled against my thigh as I typed on the computer. If we were away for more than a few hours, Max became anxious and would pick at the top of his head until it bled. Did I mention we have commonalities, this creature and me?

My husband was none too happy that I promptly retrieved Max and brought him to bed with me, putting him under my chin or on my chest. "He was abruptly separated from his mother," I explained to Larry. "He needs us to understand what has happened to him. And furthermore, you have insisted upon us having these dogs, so you will now put up with how I respond to them!"

He knew there was no sense arguing with me about this, so he rolled over and went to sleep. I'm sure he was thinking, "When am I going to have my wife back?"

Max started going in his kennel at night without crying at about three months old, finally feeling secure enough to leave Larry and me to have our bed to ourselves again. But he still stayed there with us til' it was time to actually go to sleep (still does), and always takes naps with me.

He struggles with anxiety. He is over 100 pounds now, but nobody sent him a memo about the weight gain. Although he sleeps in his kennel on a regular basis, he still has issues on nights there are thunderstorms or he is feeling anxious for some other reason. He sleeps right under my chin or plops right down on top of me, all 100-plus pounds of him. I don't mind.

When we go on vacation, Larry arranges for a sitter to stay with him at the house and spend as much time with him as possible, just sitting with him and allowing him the gift of presence. When we are away, I ask the person who cares for him to text me photos of him, particularly his head, so I can see how he's doing. (I can tell if he has been picking at his head and torn it apart. And then I tell the sitter exactly what to do to help him.)

My kids say, "Mom, you have created a monster!"

They roll their eyes at the things I will do to make sure Max is okay.

I have not created a monster. And Max is not a monster.

We understand each other quite perfectly.

In the days right after mine and Judy's falling out, I stayed in bed with Max. His big paws were around my neck, square fuzzy face and cold nose pressed against my cheek, my tears a constant fountain.

Max has heard more of this story than anybody else.

Squeaking not Speaking

I was having lunch with an adoptee friend recently and we talked about losses of any kind pertaining to your natural mother. Both of us agreed that there is absolutely nothing like it. It has the power to emotionally slay you whether you are two or 92! There is nothing like the mother-child bond. Being a person who has experienced several different kinds of pain in life and survived, I can only speak for myself that there is nothing that compares.

In the three days following the phone call, I turned to get support from the community online, a lot. But as far as verbalizing anything, most of the time I was not actually talking, I was squeaking. This is what happens when I am sobbing and trying to talk at the same time and it just doesn't work out.

Although actually "talking" about it was a challenge, my fingers worked well. I was connecting online night and day with those in the adoptee and first mother community, and they would send me their phone numbers and say, "Deanna, I'm here for you! Pick up the phone and call me..." and I would explain since they would only hear squeaks on the other end, it wouldn't be of much good. Anytime I opened my mouth to talk for the first three days, I dissolved to a pile of tears, so messaging was better. So many reached out and cared, day and night. People of every faith you can imagine, and no faith at all. Showing up 24/7 when I popped up online to say, "Is anyone there?"

Someone was always there.

My First Two Thoughts

The first thing that crossed my mind after we got off the phone was: "I'm going to have to forgive this."

I'm a believer. Real believers forgive. It was never a question in my mind that I was going to forgive her. Although I lean on God for help to do what I cannot do alone, I instinctively knew I may need the help of one of His followers with a set of letters behind his or her name, to guide me.

The second thought was: "How am I going to work?" I know that sounds bizarre. This has never happened to me before. Ever.

I was worried about work in the middle of the worst conversation of my life. As I was struggling to continue talking while in the midst of what felt like an emotional hurricane, my mind also raced to the items on my work agenda. How weird is that? I'm going to explain the significance of this in a moment.

I took a few days off from work, which was a relief, since talking without crying was a major issue.

I felt like I had been shot repeatedly with a machine gun in my upper body. My friend Kathryn always asks people, "Where do you feel it in your body?" in relation to stressful situations. I felt it like crazy. My upper body was in constant pain the first few days.

In Pursuit of Help

I began emailing local Christian counselors to try to find someone who could understand. I had given up on getting professional help for adoption related issues years ago when two Christian counselors completely dismissed adoption as having anything to do with my struggles. But, I was desperate to try again. I sent a bunch of emails, no longer than a short paragraph, explaining that I had just experienced a post-adoption related issue, and needed immediate help. The only question I asked was, "Do you have an understanding of trauma, grief, and significant loss as it relates to adoption?" I was specifically searching for a Christian counselor with competency in these areas relating to adoption.

Pursuing professional counseling when needed has always been a priority to me because neither of my mothers received the proper help they needed to thrive. It affected everything in both families. My desire and commitment has always been to pursue spiritual and emotional wholeness, not just for me but for the sake of my husband, children, and everyone that I come into contact with in the world. I believe one of the best gifts we can give those around us is a whole, healthy person.

While waiting for answers to come by email, I curled up in bed with Max, with a heating pad on my back—

moving it to my chest when needed, in an attempt to soothe the constant ache. I would read the Bible and *Jesus Calling* by Sarah Young, and pray, listen to worship music, and take long baths. The fountain of tears washed with the sudsy water that went down the drain.

I didn't want my husband to leave my side. This is not normal for me. I am not what would be described as a needy wife. At all. My husband leaves for significant periods of time if necessary for ministry purposes, etc., while I manage the household, the entire church and more, even on short notice. I travel around the world by myself, for speaking engagements. I am not afraid of solitude and, in fact, I require it to be effective. I am not the type of wife who gets upset about my husband going out with friends or colleagues, or keeps tabs on how long he is gone. But after the phone call, things were different.

Larry went to pick up his keys from off of his dresser. "Where are you going?" I panicked.

"I'm just running over to the store to get a gallon of milk and a few other things..."

"No!" I begged. "You can't leave me! Please! Have one of the boys go. Don't leave the room... come stay beside me... lay over here with Max and me..."

Larry must have wondered who stole his wife and left a toddler in her place...

I buried my face in his chest, gripping him tightly, begging him, "Don't leave me! Don't leave me! Don't leave me!"

Days Later...

"Babe, I have a board meeting tonight. You know, I am fine with you taking time off to process this and do what you need to do, but I need to keep working... I can't just lay here beside you..."

"Come right back," I said. "Don't stop on the way home. Don't go anywhere else. Just have the meeting and come straight home."

I would lie next to Max, reading or praying and count the moments until Larry got home. And, I would talk to those who were my support group online. Larry said, "Babe, I have nothing against your support group, but do you think it's good to talk to them for this many hours a day? I'm not sure this is a balanced way to handle this, and may hurt you rather than help you."

I said, "They are the only ones who really understand, completely. I'll ask a counselor, when I find one, about whether it's a healthy thing to talk to them this much right now. Or whether what I'm involved in is really the danger Judy thinks it is. For right now, they are helping me to get through this because they have a different level of understanding."

Was I praying? Yes.

God and I never lost touch, not at all.

Unfortunately a lot of people didn't get the memo that you can be in touch with God and go through hell. Followers in the New Testament were beaten, imprisoned, boiled in oil, stoned... yet they were never out of touch with Jesus.

But somehow we think if people today go through hard times and struggle, they must have lost touch with Jesus.

Unfortunately, it would get worse.

I spent the rest of the week searching for a therapist.

The Next Blow

Toward the end of the week, an e-mail came from Judy.

Oh thank God! An apology letter, I thought.

I didn't think it was a letter giving my father's name.

But, I thought for sure it would be an, "I'm sorry."

It didn't even take any faith to believe for that.

I opened it and was devastated by the contents.

No apology.

I always try to look for the "gift" in everything. This was no exception.

I was happy about two things about this letter. The first was that it actually opened up a conversation again even though it wasn't the conversation I dreamed of.

And, the second was that she said she was not going to end our relationship if I did DNA, but it was clear she never wanted to discuss it again.

I took it as an open door.

Not to ask her for the name, or press her about that, but simply to pour out my heart.

My Response

I proceeded to do what I instinctively do. I wrote. And wrote. And wrote.

When finished I had completed a six-page letter, twelve-point font, single-spaced.

Not a request for the name. (I had already accepted that this was not a possibility, from her.)

My desire was to say everything I've ever wanted to say to my mother, without holding back. Good things, loving things—anything left unsaid.

As I wrote, I felt prompted to keep this question in mind, "God forbid, if my mother would pass away tomorrow, what things would I have wished I had said?" Those were the things I wrote. This was why it took six pages.

I apologized for any pain I had brought to her, in any fashion, including my conception and delivery. (I know I don't need to apologize for these things. I did anyway.)

I explained my heart and where I was coming from to ask for his name in the first place, yet told her I had accepted that she had made her decision and was not asking again.

I hoped that maybe understanding would come.

Before sending it, I submitted the letter to my husband, and several close friends—for insight and correction. The letter brought most of them to tears. Some said, "If I received a letter like that, I would be running to my daughter's arms as quickly as I possibly could."

I sent it off, and prayed for that.

And Smack Dab into a New Rose Bush

It didn't happen.

What came back was another letter not apologizing for, but affirming everything that had already been said, and a bit more.

One of my friends said, "This latest response is gaslighting." I had no idea what that meant and had to look it up! It turns out, gaslighting is a form of mental and emotional abuse in which false information is presented with the intent of making a victim doubt his or her own memory, perception, and sanity. Instead of dealing with the issue at hand—my request for my father's name, she turned the conversation around to focus on the medical issue I was diagnosed with that is genetically linked to my paternal side. Rather than answer my request for my father's name, she promptly called me a liar because I hadn't immediately shared the diagnosis with her.

On the night of our reunion in 1991, I thanked her for "choosing life." Then I felt kind of silly when she gently turned to me and said, "I never even considered an abortion." But now in this letter, she suddenly changed her story about this too, saying that abortion *was* always an option—one I needed to be thankful she didn't choose.

Instead of focusing on my request for my father's name, she chose to turn it around to call me a liar, and to admonish me to just be thankful.

I would be advised by every person who read our letters not to respond anymore.

My initial response was to want to keep writing back and back and back, to try again. I didn't want to give up.

Godly and mature people I have placed myself in an accountable relationship with down through the years said, "Deanna, it will just keep getting worse if you continue to respond. Take some time away and heal."

I knew they were right.

Crying in My Chicken

After three days, Larry thought it might be good for me to get out of the house. I told him the only way I'd face anyone is if I could just show up, "as is." I did have to change out of my nightgown I had been living in for three days.

Our friends Gayle and David Lechner from church are the kind of people with which you can be real without fear. No pretenses. We made arrangements to meet them for dinner at Carrabbas, my favorite place.

Sitting and talking over dinner, we shared for a few hours while my tears fell in my Chicken Bryan. They were perfectly okay with me not being okay.

Something all of us need desperately is friends who are okay with us admitting that we're not okay.

Meltdown on the Highway

On the way home, my cell phone rang and it was my mother-in-love, Lydia Shrodes. I've always referred to my husband's parents as the "in-loves" instead of "in-laws" because they have been nothing but a loving support to me for all the years of our marriage. My husband often teases that he's jealous that once he married me, his parents loved me more than him. The truth is, I am the blessed one.

Larry's mother, Lydia, said she just felt in her heart that something was wrong, and called to ask if I was okay. Seeing her number on my cell phone, I froze. I was overwhelmed at the thought of talking about it. I let the call go to voicemail.

Larry said, "Babe, who called?"

Tears.

"Please talk to me."

Sobbing.

"Tell me what to do, please... what do you need me to do to help you?" he asked.

We were on the highway and he couldn't pull over.

The phone rang again. I pressed "answer" that time, but was beside myself with grief at having to speak the truth about what had just happened, out loud. What was churning inside was so deep and overwhelming and I feared unleashing it.

I was listening to Lydia's voice on the phone pouring out her love and trying to console me about whatever was wrong. But all I could do was fall forward into the dashboard, pressing my head into it, and release loud, gut-wrenching sobs. I stayed there, sobbing and alternately wanting to leap out of the moving car, and run and run and never stop running, but to where I didn't even know…

You can't just "leave" what are many times the complexities of life. Well, some people do. (Adoptees are over-represented in treatment centers and have a much higher rate of suicide.) My faith in God has sustained me through the worst of the complexities, but my heart breaks for those who have made the irretrievable choice to leave this world…those who don't know how deeply God loves them and that in Him there IS hope, healing, and a future.

My mother-in-love just wanted to take the pain away. She ranted, "I'm about to drive over to Richmond and handle this myself! This is ridiculous! Absolutely ridiculous!"

Later that night, Larry would tell her interfering at all where Judy was concerned would only bring harm, not help. She listened, aching for me, just wanting so badly to fix it.

"You've been the greatest joy to Dad and me," she spoke as she could hear me weeping. "We love you with all our hearts, and we just don't understand why this is happening."

She couldn't fix it.

I could never be good enough to fix it.

A six page, twelve-point font, single-spaced letter couldn't fix it.

Loving a person couldn't fix it.

And sometimes even when we pray our guts out, people do the opposite of what we pray for.

Even when it's a righteous prayer.

No one could fix it, and I knew that.

That's why it felt so utterly hopeless that night.

Larry pulled the car over into a Walmart parking lot.

Once I could manage to speak, I said, "I need some help."

"I know," he said.

Chapter 12— Finding Melissa

"There are wounds that never show on the body that are deeper and more hurtful than anything that bleeds."

— *Laurell K. Hamilton,* Mistral's Kiss

Searching for a Christian counselor with competency in treating post-adoption issues was proving to be about as difficult as finding a Paula Deen recipe that doesn't contain a stick of butter.

More difficult than finding a bathing suit you like the first time you try one on.

More difficult than finding a Super Walmart with all their registers open.

I continued to Google and came across a Christian counseling center in Tampa. Even though we had pastored a church in the Tampa Bay area for eleven years, I had never heard of it. That's because it was a relatively new center, just a few years old.

My heart skipped a beat when I saw the name: Restoration Counseling Center.

Would Restoration Counseling answer my e-mail in a positive way?

I sent the e-mail to the address provided at their site, and imagine my delight when therapist Melissa Richards answered my message within just a few hours. She said that YES she understood and YES she thought she would be able to help me. I was further encouraged about the fact that some of her special areas of practice include but are not limited to: adoption issues, eating disorders, grief, trauma, and more.

We set an appointment immediately for the first available time.

Catching a Ride to Therapy

Larry and I have chosen during most of the years of our marriage only to have one car because we work together at the church. Sometimes that gets challenging. During the time of my therapy appointment, he already had a commitment with Savanna Rose to take her to

McKechnie Field for Pirates spring training. They do it
every year as a special daddy-daughter time.

I didn't have a car to get to therapy, so I asked our son's
girlfriend at the time if she would give me a ride over to
Restoration Counseling Center and drop me off, and I'd
take her to lunch afterwards. She was actually excited
about it. The girl loved spending time with me. ~~And she
has a ton of friends. Really. She wasn't desperate or
anything.~~

When I took her to lunch afterwards and we were
enjoying our flatbread pizza and French fries loaded with
cheese, I said, "You know, it's important to live open. No
secrets. Like today. Here we are... I'm your boyfriend's
mom, and we're at lunch after you took me to therapy.
Some people might think that's the craziest thing they've
ever heard. But why? Why is that so crazy? Why do
people hide things? Why should I be ashamed that I'm
getting help? Why should we be afraid to talk about it?"

She agreed. ~~Popular AND smart, that girl.~~

I told her how important it is to always live true—be your
authentic self.

What a great lunch we had.

Hey, that's every young girl's dream, right? Nothing like
taking your boyfriend's mom to therapy.

No Secrets in this House

I told my kids from day one that I was going to get help, and why. ~~Crying into the dashboard may have been reason to tell them.~~

My kids were always aware of this entire story you've just read. Why should I hide the truth from my children? Throughout the years, some people advised that I was going to ruin my kids by living so openly. No topic being off limits—being able to ask anything or talk about it and getting a straight answer, sharing our honest feelings even on really difficult days.

"Some things are better left unsaid," they said. "You need to use more discretion..." "Everything doesn't need to be talked about out in the open..."

I don't agree.

Often as pastors Larry and I are asked the question, "When did you have 'the talk' with your kids?" We never had THE talk. We have a series of talks. Every day we have talks. About everything! Still do. The talks never end.

~~Give me a moment to brag please, before we move on with unpacking my meltdown.~~

At the time of this writing, Dustin is 24-years-old. He's the youth pastor at our church and a licensed minister with the Assemblies of God. You already know he's an amazing guitar player. Sings too. Everybody says, "If you've seen the mother, you've seen the son," when it comes to Dustin and me. We are so much alike, it's scary at times. I'm crazy about this guy. He's my favorite.

Jordan is 23-years-old. Yes, he and Dustin are only a year apart. He's a coordinator in the fraud department at Capital One and very good at what he does there. He's also one of the best drummers I've heard in my lifetime and has placed in competitions for drumming. He serves in worship ministries and helps out in any way that he can to assist our family or the church. I'm crazy about this guy. He's my favorite.

Savanna Rose is seventeen-years-old. She's a senior in high school. She teaches a life group for children at the church and interns at church camp during the summers, ministering to children. Loves God with all her heart. I'm crazy about this girl. She's my favorite.

So those are my kids. They seem to have fared really well with a mom who talks about everything at the dinner table from sex to therapy to the fact that sometimes life hurts.

Speaking of Therapy

From the moment I walked into Melissa's office and sat on her couch, I felt relief. The overwhelming thought I had when I entered the room for the first time was, *You are safe now.* I can't explain why I felt that. I just did.

Melissa Richards sets you at ease immediately and makes you feel as if you've been dipped in a pool of peace.

When you share with her, she has a look on her face that I can only describe as knowing down to her core exactly where you are coming from. There are times when you tell her the hardest parts of your story that her eyes moisten much more than normal, although she never loses her composure or professional demeanor.

Melissa knows the whole of my life experience—what I've written here and a lot more that I haven't shared.

I would not have wished the pain I've experienced on anyone, but one gift contained therein was that it was a trigger of such a traumatic degree that it propelled me to land in Melissa Richards' office. I am certain I would not be writing this right now as an overcomer, had I not received her help. There are people God has specifically called and anointed to help people in this regard.

Detaching

Melissa would end up spending extra time with me the first day, just to get me stabilized. One of the first things she did was share with me the importance of being what is known as regulated. ~~No, this has nothing to do with Metamucil or putting more fiber in my diet.~~

So the first priority was to become regulated, and she put me on a path to becoming so. For me, becoming regulated required: lowering my expectations of myself for a time, getting more rest, connecting with supportive people, and most of all—living in the present and refusing to detach no matter how painful things were.

When Judy and I were having the painful conversation, my mind kept veering to work, especially during the worst parts. I couldn't explain why it did that. Why were work agenda items popping up during the most difficult conversation of my life? It puzzled me. (This is one reason counseling has been so key for me. I would have never figured this out on my own!)

Melissa's first observation was that I had experienced what she referred to as, "perpetual trauma," throughout life. This is also known as complex trauma. Detaching had been my life-long response. She explained that I would detach from it in order to survive. My choice in detaching was most often working or emotional eating and binging. Detaching was the first issue we would tackle.

The optimal situation was for me to take a month off and go somewhere to rest and focus on healing. But that wasn't possible with logistics at the time.

During recovery, by the grace of God I kept up with co-pastoring the church full-time, career coaching a few hours a week, and traveling to fulfill speaking engagements.

I had been in Christian counseling before for workaholism issues, but they never connected it to post-adoption issues. As I encountered the words on the phone that rocked my world to the core, my first thought was, "How am I going to work now?" It's the first time that ever happened. I felt paralyzed and unable to function. This was foreign to me.

As Judy spoke, I was listening to her words and the more painful they got, my mind kept veering to upcoming work responsibilities. Since work was always my safe place— my escape, my mind kept trying to leave the conversation with Judy and go to my "safe place."

It wasn't working.

My overwhelming thought when considering the responsibilities was, "How am I going to work now?"

I had just been fractured and wasn't sure how I was going to function going forward. I know some people who have not been through this will not get what I'm saying.

If you are a believer, I imagine you might be thinking, "Why didn't you just turn it over to Jesus?" I know, because some people have actually said this to me.

Even a few people very close to me did not understand. So, let me explain in a way that might help you grasp it.

The Skater

Let's say you are a professional skater.

You teach at a local skating rink and are responsible for many other skaters. You also have many upcoming competitions. At least one weekend a month you are away for a skating event or competition.

Like any human, you sometimes get a headache or your muscles ache. You get indigestion here or there. No problem. You address these issues and most times they are quickly resolved, in a day or two.

But one day, the unthinkable happens. Both of your legs get broken.

You wonder, "How am I going to walk now? To skate? To teach? To work? To compete? To do anything I need to do?"

You are fractured.

Broken.

There is no denying this and you cannot wish it away.
Hope it away.

You are a skater with two broken legs.

You can pray about it.

You can turn it over to Jesus.

Jesus will help you through this... He will be by your side
to journey with you through recovery.

But the fact is: you are broken.

That was me the night of February 28.

People don't tend to have the same respect for emotional
brokenness as they do physical brokenness. Because they
can't see the broken heart like they could a broken leg,
it's easy to doubt that anything significant is really
wrong.

Considering My Commitments

I had a lot of upcoming speaking dates, traveling to
conferences and events near and far. The first weekend
conference I was scheduled to preach was coming just
two weeks after the fallout with Judy. I begged Melissa to
please just help me to get stabilized enough to fulfill my
engagements, and do a good job.

You may wonder why I didn't just call everyone and say I couldn't come. I didn't cancel because first of all, I do care about the people I'm going to speak for. Second, I know what it's like to be the leader who has invested all the money in marketing materials... made the financial investment of the posters, the flyers, had the promo videos made, and all the rest. Not to mention, it's hard to find someone else at the last minute. They have put their blood, sweat, and tears into an event. And then someone calls and says, "Something's come up. I'm not coming." That sends a leader into absolute tailspin. I know what it's like to be on the receiving end of that and it's horrible. I had never done it to anyone, and I couldn't imagine starting now, even if I was broken. I've preached with fever and chills before, just so somebody wouldn't have to panic. My plan was to put accepting any more speaking invitations outside the church on hold for a while, but I wanted to at least fulfill the ones I had committed to.

A Virus? A Sickness? Dangerous?

I asked Melissa's opinion about the adoptee community as well as presenting Larry's question to her about how much time I should be spending turning to my online support.

Melissa affirmed that my support group was not a virus or a sickness. She validated that this was a safe place for me to turn to. In the early days of recovery she said I should go there as much as I felt the need to, as many hours of the day as I wanted. Having this kind of a safe place was very important to my recovery. It would become a reasonable amount of time as I progressed. As recovery continued, she said my time spent receiving support from the online community would not be excessive and come into balance. And it did.

Am I Crazy?

I kept waiting for Melissa to tell me I was crazy. She never did.

Over the months of recovery she would come to tell me, "Deanna, you have issues that need to be worked on. You do need to be here. And truthfully everyone has issues to work on. However, I want you to know that especially with the trauma and significant loss you have been through, you're rather amazing." Again and again she would encourage me about my resilience.

I often wondered if she was just being nice to me in my fragile condition, waiting until I got stronger to tell me I was crazy. Imagine my surprise when months later she would ask if she could publish one of my adoption writings on her counseling website to help clients who were in therapy. She also went on to do a published interview with me on the subject of complex trauma.

Sorting Truth from Lies

When Judy first shared with me on February 28 that she was "basically raped," I was advised by someone I deeply respect that I had no choice but to believe her, accept the fact that I was conceived from rape, and take this as my new "updated and revised" life story.

I don't have a problem accepting this if it is true.

I just don't know what's true, because I've been told several conflicting stories, by Judy herself.

I don't know which one to believe and still have more questions than answers.

I'm not making any dogmatic statements… just wondering.

I do believe that my mother's continued use of "basically" may have been used because she may have *felt* raped, regardless. Perhaps my father pursued younger women, had sex with them, and left them with no intention of helping them if they got pregnant. And it's quite possible that he was arrogant, uncaring, or even cruel afterwards.

If that is the case and it was consensual sex, it doesn't make him a rapist, but it does make him a jerk. There is a difference.

Rapist or jerk? I don't know.

Maybe I'll never know.

I do know in any case that he was a painful part of my mother's past.

He could be a rapist, he could be a jerk, or he could be neither.

No matter who and what he is, he is one of the two human beings I come from. I have carefully considered what the person whom I deeply respect had told me: that I must now accept my mother's story, and I absolutely must not question it.

Do I have to accept Judy's determination at face value? Am I wrong to question whether she is lying, since by her own admission she has done so on this issue several times? Was I guilty of "blaming the victim," my very own mother, whom I love deeply? Or, is it possible instead to accept that Judy has given me various versions of the story, to choose not to judge, and to move forward with my plan to find my natural father?

As one adoptee so eloquently said, "I don't want to pass judgment on the circumstances of my conception. I just want to know who was there at the time."

I'm Not an Isolated Case

In being connected to scores of people in the adoptee community the past few years, I've met quite a number of people who share a similar story to mine. There are adoptees who never heard the word "rape" until they pressed the issue of wanting to know their father's name. When a mother uses the word "rape," she automatically assumes there will be no further questions, or searching.

Although it would pain me greatly to know that my mother, or anyone in my life, was harmed in any way, it was not this that drove me to go to counseling. I can accept the truth—no matter how tragic it may end up to be. If I was conceived from rape, I can come to terms with that. I know my worth; I know who God has called me to be—no matter how I was conceived.

It is the lies that have been the hardest to accept and sometimes feel impossible to accept.

I am not sure what to believe because on all of the occasions we have ever spoken about my father, my mother told me the same thing: that she lied.

Lies are the one consistent thing about my history.

~~I am now allergic to lies.~~

Getting Power

Many adoptees I know seem to struggle with control issues because many who made the decisions for us in childhood continue to try to do so even into our adulthood. We are treated as perpetual children by our natural or adoptive parents at times—and furthermore by unjust laws that keep us from having our factual certificate of birth, medical histories, and more. It's important to note that all of this information is not unknown. We are simply prohibited from having our personal information because of uncooperative individuals, archaic laws, or in my case—both.

One day when I was feeling powerless over all of the above and more, Melissa asked me to make a list of the ways I could get power. Some things were along the lines of connecting with God and leaning on Him for power, but I also had the ability to make choices for myself. One of those was the choice to pursue DNA testing. Melissa fully supported me in making this empowering decision for myself and prayerfully awaited the results with me.

To my surprise—I didn't have to pay for even one of my three DNA tests! I never asked anyone to help me. But, three friends who do not even know one another and live in three different areas of the world each felt led to approach me and tell me they wanted to pay for a DNA test. There were three tests to take, and three friends spoke up and financially provided them. It was all quickly taken care of. God knows exactly what we need when we need it. I stand amazed at how He shows His care for me.

Speaking of that...

The Dream Team

The day after the phone call with Judy, Priscilla Sharp reached out and messaged me to offer support. Priscilla is a first mother, with a heart of compassion wider and deeper than the Grand Canyon. She is world renowned for her work as a Search Angel, with hundreds of successes under her belt. Priscilla reached out to me in the days right after my fallout with Judy, and before she did anything else, cried with me. Then she said, "Deanna, when you're ready, I'm willing. I will do my best to find your natural father."

Then, shortly after Priscilla approached me, Gaye Tannenbaum reached out. She's known for her expertise with DNA. "If you want me on your team, count me in," she said. I could hardly believe that I had been so blessed to be offered these two women's assistance!

Again, I stood amazed at God's provision.

Laura's Revelation

One of my favorite things to do when we're both lucky enough to have the time available is to lie on the hammock on my patio and talk to Laura Dennis on the phone. Most people in the adoptee and first parent community are already acquainted with Laura—she's a well-known adoptee blogger. We've become very close friends over the past few years. Even though she lives in Serbia we have regular phone calls due to the technology of MagicJack.

One day Laura brought up an important revelation. She mentioned that she noticed that my crying had tapered off within five days after my conversation with Judy. Remember... the first three days it was practically 24/7, then five hours on the fourth day and three hours on the fifth. She asked me "How much are you crying now?"

I said, "Well, just intermittently... depends on the day. And not even every single day anymore. It hits me at certain moments."

She said, "Deanna, remember the second time you lost Judy after the confidential intermediary situation, how you cried every night for two years?"

I said, "Yes..."

She said, "What is the difference between the aftermath of that loss and this one?"

We both agreed that the third loss felt worse having been in active relationship with Judy for twenty years and having so much more to lose. Yet in a mere five days, my crying was improved, even before I started counseling! Why was this?

Laura noted that back then, although I was turning to God, I wasn't connected to the community.

Community was the missing component, and it makes all the difference!

God has wired us to need community. We aren't meant to walk alone. I cried every night for two years without reprieve because I was not connected to others walking the same road who could lift me up. I needed them, and they needed me.

Without this amazing group of adoptees and first moms, I'd still be crying. We need to reach out, to be a part of what God has provided for us.

I would soon be grateful for the community at a whole new level, because June 6th was soon to give February 28th a run for its money.

Chapter 13—
The Call I Never Expected

"Many people pray to be kept out of unexpected problems.

Some people pray to be able to confront and overcome them."

— *Toba Beta,* Betelgeuse Incident

Melissa said I was one of the only clients ever that she didn't give homework to. She said the last thing I needed on my plate was more work.

I had asked about books to read, things to study, or assignments to fulfill before our next appointment. I'm the type of person who always has a list, and knows exactly where I'm headed to get the job done.

But Melissa said no, I didn't need another list of things to do, and that I was to do absolutely nothing but grieve.

In fact she said I would be grieving for quite a while— moving through all of the stages of grief.

She constantly encouraged me to give it time.

"Sit in this and be sad. Give yourself permission to feel it," she said.

Aside from things on my agenda for work that absolutely had to be done, she counseled me to sit in the sadness. "Your homework is to be sad," she said.

It was time for me to move beyond the old habits of detaching from my pain by working, emotional or binge eating, or other destructive means of responding. (Just to clarify, work is not destructive. Work is actually a God-given blessing. But, it can be abused or misused, like anything else.)

My Sister's First Call

About a week after mine and Judy's conversation, my sister called to ask about what had happened, from my point-of-view. I could only assume she had heard about it from Judy, since I hadn't said a word. We have become so close over the years, able to talk about anything. But I didn't want to put a wedge between her and our mother, or between her and I. The last thing I wanted to do was put my sister in the middle. I felt that would be very unfair to her.

When she called to ask about things, I told her that while I don't keep secrets as a rule, I thought it was wisdom that we didn't discuss the falling out, so as to preserve Judy's relationship with both of us. She agreed and thought that was a great idea. We prayed together without sharing any details and hung up. I was elated that my relationship with my sister was intact and would not be affected by what had happened.

Adjusting My View

Through counseling, I came to realize many things that affected me in not healing from the past. The first was an adjustment I needed to make in the way I viewed the forgiveness and reconciliation process as it relates to trauma. I had always thought that it was unhealthy, not to mention unbiblical, to not get over anything that happens to you, immediately. It was the whole, "Don't let the sun go down on your wrath" biblical principle. I have come to realize, dealing with wrath is different from recovering from complex trauma. I wasn't after revenge, I just wanted relief.

I believe there are three stages of forgiveness: the will to forgive, the process of forgiveness, and then the state of forgiveness. You decide to forgive someone as an act of your will. Then you go through a process in your heart of working through things, and finally you come to the point of living in the state of forgiveness. The Lord has helped me go through that process so many times.

This time, I struggled with guilt that the process was taking more time, primarily because it had to do with my mother. Though I willed in my heart to forgive her even in the midst of the painful conversation, and even after receiving the two painful letters, the process was taking time. I was not emotionally ready to reach out again, for a while. And I had no idea when I'd be ready.

Melissa explained to me, I was still actively in-process—moving toward healing and forgiveness, but it was going to take time. Just because I hadn't yet reconciled with Judy and spoken to her yet, didn't mean I wasn't going to. The deeper traumas are, the more time it takes to move forward. In my case I was moving forward, not only from the recent situation with Judy, but also from other unresolved issues connected to my adoption.

There were moments I felt horrible that it was taking a significant amount of time. I would come to realize what I was dealing with was guilt, which is not of God. Conviction of the Holy Spirit moves us to make changes God wants us to make, but guilt doesn't come from Him. I would just imagine myself reaching out to call her number or writing a letter, and I would dissolve to a pile of tears. I felt guilty for feeling that way, though I couldn't identify the reason for the guilt except that taking time to talk to somebody again, especially my mother, just didn't feel right. I learned that much of the grace I extended to others, I didn't give to myself. That needed to change.

"You're just not ready," Melissa would say. "And that's okay. Can I invite you to take the time clock out of this process and allow yourself to take as much time as it takes to recover?"

I took comfort in the fact that in scripture, all were not healed instantly. Some were, as scripture says, "Healed as they went."

Through Melissa's gentle guidance I came to realize the importance of respecting the process and not skipping over any steps that God had for me to take on my journey of healing.

The First Conference

The first weekend conference I was scheduled to preach was in two weeks. I had been following all of Melissa's counsel in moving forward. Although I was still working, I took the recovery process very seriously. I would set time aside to sit in the sadness and grieve. Or, I would do work that didn't require a lot of brain power and spend time grieving. Things like pulling weeds in the yard. I'd go out, pull weeds, and cry for a few hours. ~~Yes, there are that many weeds in my yard.~~

Larry drove me to the first conference because I didn't have the strength to make the drive. He took me to the city where I was preaching, making a stop first at my favorite restaurant in the area to have a quiet dinner with me. Afterwards we got an ice cream cone and went and sat in a park. Popping the point of the sugar cone in and wiping the corners of my mouth, I buried my head in his chest and held on for a long time as we sat there.

Sliding my hands inside his leather jacket and pulling myself as tight to him as I could...

"I don't want you to leave," I whispered.

But he had to leave.

He had to be back at the church.

This would be our first time apart since February 28.

I knew God was going to do some amazing things that weekend, because whenever we're at our weakest that's when He shows up all the more.

I threw myself into helping others that weekend and just hoped they wouldn't ask much about me.

The weekend went amazing, by the grace of God.

Even so, I counted the very minutes until Larry pulled up to get me and take me home.

Questions from the Kids

My children had been extremely supportive, trying to understand and comfort. At the same time, they were hurting too. They knew everything. And they were sad.

In March we had our usual family dinner at Kobe for Jordan's birthday and we sat around the table for a long time talking. No topic has ever been of limits, whether times are good or bad. They brought up the situation and asked some questions.

Things like, "Are we still Greek?"

"I don't know. There's a lot of things I don't know anymore and I'm sorry for that. I wish I had more answers for you."

The institution of adoption in its current form not only affects the adoptee, it affects the adoptee's children.

"I miss Pop Pop Tom," said Dustin.

The kids love Grandma Judy but they loooooooooooooooooooove "Pop Pop Tom" as they have called him for twenty years.

He had played a game with the boys that very first night in 1993 and won their hearts. They would go on to play many games over the years on our visits. Tom also has a special gift for finding the perfect gifts for special people in his life. You never know when one of these presents from Tom is going to pop up in your mailbox. It's not about expense or extravagance—it's the thought and care he puts into finding such unique things. He's so much fun and knows everything about everything. We have often said if any of us were ever on the show, *Who Wants to Be a Millionaire*, and needed to phone a friend, we'd call Tom. You can ask a question about a rare spider in the tropics and he will tell you all about it. I call him the "walking encyclopedia."

"I miss Pop Pop Tom too, and Grandma Judy," I said, "but I don't know when I'm going to be ready."

I encouraged the kids to contact them. To see them when we stopped through on our summer vacation, even if I wasn't ready yet.

"That's awkward, Mom. It's just not the same without you."

"I know," I said. "I'm sorry about that, but right now it just is what it is."

Can't You Just Snap Out of it and Move On?

Melissa was encouraging me to take time to heal, but some others, not so much. A few months into the process my sister called again and said she couldn't handle the pressure of what had happened between our mother and me. I was puzzled by why she was so upset since first of all, we had no discussion about the falling out. I had shared absolutely nothing with her about the situation up to that point, in an effort to protect her. I learned she was under pressure because she was hearing a lot about it from our mother.

My sister expressed strong disagreement with the process taking time. She wanted it to be quickly resolved and felt like this was the only proper spiritual response. Surely Jesus would not want me to take so much time before reaching out again to my mother. I shared that I was in counseling and to recover properly it had to be at the pace I could handle, not the one others expected of me.

I also shared with her that I had written our mother a six-page letter pouring my heart out and said everything I had to say. I had nothing more to say to her at the time, and all that was left for me to do right now was heal. I even said, "God forbid if something were to happen to her tomorrow, I've said all that I need to say."

She was not altogether comfortable and expressed it, but at the end of the conversation she seemed to understand that stronger boundaries were needed so that she didn't have to be under pressure. We agreed to disagree about my recovery process and it seemed things were okay between us. I was relieved. The last thing I wanted was to lose my sister or my brother.

Listening Prayer

Things were approaching four months.

I was feeling stronger daily, yet still working through the anger stage of grief.

One morning I was taking Max and Maddie out to walk and I felt so guilty that I was almost four months out and still processing so much and not at the point where I could handle picking up the phone. I literally said aloud, "God, are you truly okay with this?"

I'm sure if somebody was walking by and overheard, they may have thought, *Yeah lady... God is okay with you walking two dogs.*

Mother's Day came and I was emotionally unable to call. I sent a card. However, with our state ministers district council the next day, having decorating responsibilities for a women's ministry luncheon there, and then leaving before the council was even over to fly to North Carolina to preach for a few days, I feared calling Judy. I knew in my heart I was not strong enough and did not want to be distracted from the responsibilities at hand. A card had to suffice.

Sitting in our session the next week I said, "Melissa, I've gotten some pressure to resolve this quicker and aside from external pressure from others, I'm feeling internal pressure."

Once more, she identified it as guilt.

"Deanna, we're going to practice listening prayer right now. We're both going to pray, in silence. You're going to ask God, "How long is okay? How long is acceptable for this to last?" While you're praying, I'm going to pray for you."

Closed eyes.

Silence.

Melissa's office smells so good.

Even the smell of the place is healing.

Breathe in.

Breathe out.

Listen.

Five minutes.

Maybe ten.

I sensed God saying, "As long as it takes, Deanna. As long as it takes."

When I opened my eyes, Melissa said, "Did you hear anything from the Lord?"

"Yes, I did. He said let it take as long as it takes," I said.

"Okay," she said, "then let's do that."

And then... The Unexpected

I was gone for about a third of the month of May, away from Tampa, preaching.

I came back from my last trip, full from what the Lord did, especially in my weakness, and looking forward to having a more normal schedule—able to concentrate on home, church, and the recovery process.

My sister messaged me on the morning of Tuesday, June fourth, asking to set a time to talk with me late that afternoon. I was concentrating on church work all day and a coaching call scheduled before evening, but told her I'd be available and what time to call. I knew it probably wasn't good being that she wanted to actually schedule it. When my sister calls for pleasant things, she just calls and doesn't request to schedule anything.

I braced myself, thinking maybe she was going to press me to interrupt the recovery process again.

I could never in my wildest dreams imagine what was going to come next.

She called at the time we agreed on and quickly got to the point.

The Unthinkable

"Deanna, I know you and Mom aren't talking right now, but I needed to call and let you know this. Mom suddenly became ill yesterday. Upon running tests at the hospital, they found a mass in her liver. She is scheduled for surgery Thursday. I just wanted to let you know."

Oh. My.

I didn't want to jump to conclusions. It wasn't definite yet that she had cancer. But certainly I was concerned about the possibility.

I was extremely saddened by the news, but still very much feeling like I wasn't ready to pick up the phone.

I thanked my sister for calling and I consoled her about the news.

I listened to her thoughts and fears.

Comforted as best I could.

Tried to help her work through and process challenges she was having about the news.

She was quieter than usual.

I could tell she was upset that I was talking all about supporting her, going on and on about her, but saying little about our mother.

It may sound terrible, but honestly—I didn't know what to say.

Contrary to what some may think I don't always know what to say.

She asked me to pray.

It has been our custom to do that at the end of every call anyway.

I prayed first, and then she prayed.

But I could tell she was absolutely devastated that I didn't immediately pipe up and say, "I'm calling her, right now!"

We hung up and I knew she was extremely disappointed in me.

I tried not to think about the what-ifs.

But they were there.

I did pray.

I prayed hard.

I thought of a sermon I heard preached by another pastor that was called "Where Do I Put My Anger While I Say My Prayers?"

That was me at the moment.

Thursday. The Day Everything Changed.

June sixth came and it had already been a challenging day.

Amidst our work day, the car broke down in the pouring rain.

A tornado warning came and we were alerted to get in the closet and take shelter. We got home by a miracle with a good friend from church rigging our car up with a temporary fix.

After coming home we got freshened up for that night's sectional minister's meeting.

When I got home, Tom's voice was on the answering machine.

He was sobbing.

He said, "It's not good Deanna, it's not good. Please call me. Please, please call me."

I took a moment to breathe, dialed the number and waited for him to answer, heart pounding out of my chest.

"Hello?"

"Tom, it's Deanna..."

He broke down immediately.

"It's not good, Deanna.

Your mother has cancer.

It was a very large mass—the majority of her liver.

And they could not get it all.

Her condition is dire...

The prognosis is not good..."

More tears.

"Tom, I am so sorry. I don't know what to say, except that I'm so sorry. Sorry for you. Sorry for her. I'm so sorry…"

More tears.

"Haven't heard from you in a while, Deanna."

More tears.

"I know, Tom. I've been getting help to work through everything."

More tears.

"I heard something about that, and I'm sorry about all that. I miss hearing from you."

More tears.

"I know. I'm working through..."

More tears.

"She's in recovery but I expect they will allow calls in a few hours."

More tears.

Deep breath.

This is going to sound cruel when I say this to him.

I know it's going to sound terrible.

And maybe it is terrible.

It's going to hurt him in the midst of what is surely one of the worst—if not the worst, nights of his life.

I am going to say it as sweet as sugar, but it's going to still taste like poison.

I know this.

The war in my mind:

Deanna, don't be a terrible person. Just do whatever you are asked to do.

Deanna, stand up for yourself. It's time you are true to you.

Deanna, just give in. They need you to do as they are asking.

Deanna, stop giving in. It's always you who has to adjust.

These voices scream back and forth in my head.

Just like they have all my life.

I'm so over shoving my feelings down, even if it is life-and-death.

I am devastated upon hearing the report of her condition.

And I am still slayed by what happened months ago.

I can't just snap out of it, as much as I wish I could.

I am feeling overwhelming grief.

For what happened four months previous... for the fact that she has cancer... for everything.

It's simply overwhelming, these feelings, and I just want to go outside and run.

And run.

And run.

I want to get off the phone and run.

To where, I don't even know.

Another deep breath.

"Tom, I don't know that I'm ready. I know this is huge, so huge. I am so sad. But I'm sorry, I'm just not ready tonight."

More tears.

"I just want to say one thing Deanna. I have to go because I'm crying so much, it's all running together, but I just want to say one thing and then I have to go for now."

I couldn't imagine what this would be.

I was bracing.

He went on...

"Recently, I looked up my grandmother's house on Google Maps.

You know she was special to me...

Being at her house meant so much.

I looked it up and was shocked to see, the house has been razed to the ground and the property is now just an empty lot.

There's nothing for me to go back to now. Nothing, it's all gone."

More tears.

Rivers of tears from Tom, from me.

The sounds of both our sorrow not hidden from either.

"Once something's gone, Deanna, you can't go back. You can't go back home."

I heard the sounds of his grief trailing off as he hung up.

Chapter 14—
Bringing It to Present Day

"Most people want to be circled by safety, not by the unexpected. The unexpected can take you out. But the unexpected can also take you over and change your life. Put a heart in your body where a stone used to be."

— *Ron Hall*

As soon as we hung up, I began to weep uncontrollably.

Larry wasn't available, so I went to Dustin and cried on his shoulder.

After a few minutes of telling him the devastating news, he asked what I was going to do.

"I don't know son... I don't know. I am just numb right now, but I am going to think it through tonight and pray about it. Thankfully, I already have counseling scheduled for tomorrow..."

"Mom, you know what I think?"

"What?"

"I just want to tell you...she didn't mean the stuff she said back in February..."

"She didn't?"

"No, Mom. People say the truest thing the first time. That night back in 1993 when we went to her house and you showed up and surprised her, she didn't know what to say. You caught her off guard, and she blurted out the truth. She's had twenty years to think about it, twenty years to make up something else. And when you wrote the e-mail and asked about your father, she had time to get upset about it, and then say things she didn't mean as the conversation got more uncomfortable. She knew you were coming this time. And back in 1993, she had no idea. I believe the first thing people say, especially when it's spontaneous, is the truest thing they know. I believe you need to hold on to the truth of what happened back then Mom..."

"Really?"

"Yeah. I think that's what's true."

"I hope so, Dust."

He patted my hand, long fingers that looked so much like mine, just longer...

Other arm around my shoulder, drew me in.

I cried harder and he thought it was all about Judy, but my tears were partly about the amazing wisdom I heard from one who came from me, despite all my shortcomings.

He is wise, this boy.

Well yes... this man.

And he had thought this through.

We are both people with faith a mile high.

But I think he's on to something here, not just blind faith.

Something deeper.

"I love you, Mom. It's going to be okay. No matter what, I know it's going to be okay."

The three of us had to get ready to go our minister's meeting.

I would wash my face and reapply makeup three times.

In the days to come I would stop wearing eye make-up altogether.

Reaching Out to the Church

Many people would ask me, "How do your church people feel about you writing blog posts about this and being so open?"

Our church people love me and accept me as I am. This didn't happen overnight, though.

After pastoring in Maryland for ten years, Larry and I sensed God's leading to pastor an Assembly of God church in the Tampa Bay area. Voted unanimously as the pastors, we knew we were headed for a challenge as the church had experienced much turmoil and several splits, particularly in the year just previous to us assuming the pastorate. But nothing could have prepared us for what we faced just a few days before our arrival as the new pastors. The church secretary called as we were packing up our house to move, and her screams were so dreadful, I can still hear them in my head. One of the prominent female members of the church, a choir member, was murdered right after choir practice the night before. Having lived with her husband (also a member of the church) in a situation of well-documented domestic violence, the murder rocked the church to its absolute core.

Larry and I walked into a scarred and hurting congregation, just a week later. It would take every ounce of what love and leadership we had to offer to get the church back on its feet. That labor of love continues today. One of my husband's first duties as the new lead pastor was to talk to the press, designate "media rows" in service, and make funeral arrangements. Looking back, I am amazed at the grace of God in making it through that time and the years to come.

The task of turning the church around from traumatic, multiple, and complex setbacks has been the greatest pastoral challenge of our lives. But, I see how God in His provision equipped us uniquely for the task of bringing a church through the deepest significant losses they had ever experienced to where they are today.

One of the things God spoke to Larry and me in our first days at the church was, "Don't try to change them, just love them." Our task was to throw our arms around a grieving church, not turn them upside down with a bunch of change.

I wouldn't wish the losses I have experienced on anyone; however I do see how God has utilized my pain and loss to help others, including our precious Tampa congregation. God doesn't cause everything that happens to us, but I know He will use it for His glory and our good if we allow Him to. The church in Tampa had experienced complex trauma, significant loss, and complicated grief. They now had a pastoral team who understood something about that, having experienced it personally ourselves in various forms.

It was difficult for the church to get beyond the multiple losses and establish a fresh name in the community, one that was not known for loss, but for life. In an effort to rebrand and keep the focus on current blessings and not be labeled by our past, we completely re-launched the church in January of 2010. Now Celebration Church Tampa (AG), the church, is known as a place where people can belong, believe, and become all God has created them to be.

Christians are not exempt from pain and trials. Life is sometimes complicated. And God is faithful to meet us in the midst of complexities.

Calling on the Prayer Warriors

On the evening that Tom called me about Judy's diagnosis, I wrote a private message to all of the women of our church, asking them to pray for me, and for our family. We have a private Facebook page just for the women and teen girls of our church and I shared the need with them. Many of them started reaching out and praying, although I hadn't shared any of the details yet. I knew I could count on them to lift up the need and take it seriously.

I would later gather with the women and teen girls for a special evening to share the whole story with them face-to-face. They surrounded me with love, just as I expected they would.

I find that being real brings people closer to you, not further away.

They do not seem to disrespect me because I am vulnerable with what I am going through. I sense the honesty draws people in, and they feel even safer to follow you—knowing you can admit you are not perfect. You are broken at times. You are a leader but also a fellow traveler on the journey of life.

Am I Sorry I Reunited?

Non-adoptee friends have asked me, "Are you sorry you opened up the whole can of worms of reunion? With Judy? With the subject of your father? DNA?

No. No. No. And No.

A thousand times no.

Never would I regret asking for the truth.

Never would I regret searching.

Why would I ever regret pursuing truth?

I'm the owner of the truth, even if I don't have all of it yet.

Even if I never have it.

It saddens me that asking for the truth can bring pain to others, and specifically that it brought pain to Judy. But I know it would be my deepest regret to not ask for the truth again.

For me, it's so clear—Jesus is truth. He is everything that is light and openness. Why would I want to stay in the dark? I don't understand why people think being unaware of the truth brings any glory to God.

Having knowledge of one's original family is also important for medical reasons. My mother died of the same cancer that took her father's life. I need to be vigilant about my health in this regard. A yearly physical and routine blood work did not reveal this for my mother. Had I not reunited with my mother, I would have no awareness of the need to watch for other symptoms. Reuniting has quite possibly saved my life and made it possible to live to see my children get married and know my future grandchildren. Being given my mother's medical history that she gave to the adoption agency when she was nineteen-years-old would not have sufficed.

I wonder about what I don't know concerning my father's health history. It is troublesome that at every doctor's appointment, I need to explain all over again, "I don't know the answer to that—I'm adopted." Over and over again I have to write on intake forms: "Adopted." Obviously it's important to know one's maternal and paternal history, otherwise doctors wouldn't ask about it on most every medical visit.

Opponents of equal rights for adoptees cannot see that lack of adoption rights reform can literally mean life or death for an adoptee.

Recently at my doctor's office I saw an ad for a drug that said: "If you can talk about it, you can treat it!"

I thought to myself, "If you don't know about it in the first place, you can't treat it!"

Am I living in fear about getting the same kind of cancer? No.

Now that I know, I am going to be proactive, and trust the Lord with my future.

The truth is, adoption is complex whether in reunion or not.

People are not so good with complexities.

We want it all tied up, nice and neat.

Clichés.

Pat answers.

You can "give it over to Jesus," and sometimes it still hurts like crazy.

The good news is, Jesus is right there to cry with you.

Not to tell you to snap out of it.

Jesus loves us, so much.

Sleeping on It...

I had the night to sleep on it and more than that, to pray about it.

I came to some conclusions in the night, but wanted to get Melissa's wisdom.

The phone call with Tom ripped my heart out, but I felt that taking 24 hours to process things after hearing the news was reasonable.

"Oh my. You're not wearing make-up today. Not a good sign," Melissa said as I came in and took a seat.

I proceeded to tell her the situation.

"I'm so sorry, Deanna."

I cried more tears in her office that day than on any other day.

"What do you want to do in response to this latest development?" Melissa asked.

I explained that I had considered it and prayed about it most of the night.

"I can continue the recovery process and refuse to take the risk of coming closer to her again until I'm ready. But by then, she may be gone. And it will be too late. I may have regrets, and I won't be able to do anything about it then."

"Okay," Melissa nodded as I blew my nose and swiped a few more tissues out of the box.

"Or, I can call her, I can go to her. I can get hurt again, which by all indications in our last few communications will happen—even though I'm not going to bring up what happened or discuss my father. I can tell her I love her and I'm going to forgive her, which I will do, although I'm not recovered yet. I can have closure with her—and whether a miracle happens and she lives, or whether she passes away, I will then have the rest of my life to heal."

Melissa's facial expression told me she was not surprised.

"That's exactly what I thought you would say," she said. "This is the conclusion I would have expected you to come to, knowing you as I've come to over these past few months."

More tissues from the box.

"What is hardest for you in this moment?" she asked.

Choking out the words slowly one by one, I said, "Probably the fact that a few months ago my mother said she didn't care about my pain and didn't want to hear about it. And now I'm supposed to care about hers...

I know it's cancer.

It's huge.

It's life and death.

Yet—being the one who is expected to stay in step with everyone else's desires but mine, adjusting to others' expectations and quickly moving on, putting aside what I feel for a lifetime—is overwhelming.

But I know if I don't go to her, the regret will probably be enormous.

I don't have a lot of time to keep figuring this out."

"Deanna, I want to tell you something now that you've told me your thoughts. I would support you whether you called, whether you didn't. Whether you stayed. Whether you went. After all you've been through, it's perfectly reasonable to do whatever you want to do. I'll support you. Your mother told you she didn't care. But something I've come to know about you is that you DO care about people. You care about their pain. You care about them very much. And if you call her, Deanna, if you go to her—it's not about who she is. It's about who YOU are. This is who you are. And calling, and going, and ultimately forgiving—it's a gift you give to yourself."

I felt so empowered as she said this.

Still hurting.

But empowered that I could make a choice based upon my values, not upon what others do or do not do.

God had been speaking to me about choices.

The Bike Ride

I ride my bicycle a lot. It's a pink cruiser. On the days right after February 28, I skipped riding for a few days because I was in bed.

The first day I went back out to ride, I did so for six miles while blubbering the entire time.

The adoption world talks about nature vs. nurture, and how we are all a product of both.

I was riding along and I said, "God what am I a product of? Nature has failed me. Nurture has failed me. Where did I come from? I feel as though I didn't come from earth, like I just dropped out of the sky. Nothing about where I came from makes any sense. So help me out here."

I told some friends that my plan was to throw myself a party for my next birthday and declare a rebirth. People in the church have called me Wonder Woman for years. I have so much memorabilia in my office and home. Pajamas and mugs and lunch boxes and all kinds of stuff people have given me out of love. I said they might as well make it official since my earthly identity is up in the air. They could wheel me in as I hid in a giant egg, like Lady Gaga at the Grammys years ago. I would crack open the egg, popping out in a Wonder Woman costume

singing, "Born This Way," and declare my rebirth as
Wonder Woman, descended from heaven, since I can't
get a straight answer about where I come from on earth.

Comedy is often my coping mechanism as anyone who
reads my writings very long can see. Friends laugh
profusely at the silly stuff like this that I say, but the truth
is, I have sometimes felt like an alien, like I didn't come
from earth. I know I am not alone in feeling this. Many
adoptees say they struggle with feeling like they don't
actually exist. Among other reasons, it is because they
don't know the identity of their biological parents, or
because they don't have the real piece of paper (OBC)
bearing the correct information about their birth, a
document that everyone else who is not adopted
possesses.

Everything was broken.

My adoptive home broke apart in dysfunction and
divorce.

My natural father is evidently a "monster," according to
Judy.

Possibly a rapist.

My natural mother and I are at a horrible impasse.

Everything I come from... broken apart.

God spoke back to me as I was blubbering along on my
bike and said, "Everything is not limited to nature and
nurture. There are choices. You have made choices along
the way that brought you to where you are today. Aside
from nature, nurture, and choices, there is also the

supernatural. I am God Almighty and even the elements of nature have to bow to Me. I have the ability to work outside of nature and nurture. I can do a supernatural work, particularly in anyone who is willing for Me to do so in their lives. You are a supernatural work, Deanna."

I have held onto that.

And I've held on to the ability to make good choices.

"I have full confidence in you," Melissa said. "And when you get off the phone with her, or you come back from Richmond, I will be right here to help you pick up the pieces."

Calling Tom Back

I called Tom and wasn't surprised at all when the first thing out of his mouth was, "How are you holding up?"

That's Tom.

Always thinking of others.

My husband has told me all along that he believed there was no way Tom knew the details of the falling out. "There's just no way he has any idea what you've been through," Larry has insisted over and over again. "I just can't believe that he knows the details."

I had never contacted Tom to ask about whether he knew, or requested him to interfere in any way during the previous four months.

It wasn't my place.

I believed his place was with my mother, by her side, as her husband.

But now he had contacted me and hoped I would hop right back into active relationship with her especially under the dire circumstances. I'm sure he thought I was crazy to not have responded differently. I would think that too, if I didn't know any details.

"Tom, I'm sure my reaction last night was strange," I said. "And I do not want to go into a lot of detail because we're talking about your wife here, not just my mother. But I just want to ask you a question. Were you there the night she called me?"

He said no, she chose to make the call in private.

He had no idea of the details of our conversation.

He had no idea of anything beyond that I had asked for my father's name, she had declined, and things were "a bit tense."

A bit tense? ~~Okay, yeah, that's like comparing the events of 9/11 to a bad hair day.~~

I explained just enough for him to know what landed me on Melissa's couch.

He responded just as I expected he would, with a total outpouring of grace and compassion, while still remaining loyal to Judy.

On the Other Hand...

It's was extremely hard for my sister to accept my
reaction and the process of recovery. I explained that
there were no easy fixes, even with Judy being sick.

Barring a miracle of God, she was preparing to lose her
mother.

This was a very confusing time for her to say the least.

She was scared.

She was feeling sad.

I had already lost our mother three times, so I understood
more than she realized.

A New Perspective

Once I explained a little bit about why I reacted as I did,
Tom had new understanding.

Since my call the next day after her surgery, we talked for
many hours, keeping in touch on a constant basis about
Judy's condition.

Tom is well-informed about what Judy and millions of
other young ladies went through. He has taken the
initiative to read a lot about it over the years in an effort
to understand. He recognized the pain Judy was in and
longed for her to be healed, which was one reason he
welcomed me in as he did in 1993.

I explained to him that for the past few months I didn't know what to believe.

I didn't want my new truth to be what was said on the phone on February 28—that everything was fake, or that she was sorry I found her—among other things.

"Deanna, what's true is what you experienced that night back in 1993. What was said a few months ago was the past talking. It was shame and hurt and unresolved pain talking! Don't take it into your heart. Your mother bears the scars of 1966 like a scarlet letter of sorts, the scars from society, not from you. The truth is, she has never gotten over the horrors of what happened back then. It was about how her father, society at large, ministers, and others responded to her situation. These girls were the outcasts of society. It's just the way it was back then. This isn't you, Deanna."

My voice breaking, I answered...

"I want to believe that, so much."

"Believe it. Your mother loves you. Years ago she shared with me that your relinquishment was the single most difficult thing she ever had to do. And yes, she had to. She was told by everyone around her there was no other choice. That's reality. She received this treatment because she was a young lady who stepped out of line, away from the expectations of her family and society as a whole."

I wept and thanked him over and over for his insight into this.

I believe in my heart, he is right.

Conversations with Tom also helped me gain perspective on my conversations with my mother about my history.

One day when we were talking about my ongoing search for my father, he said to me, "Deanna, I don't know if you're ever going to find through DNA because your father isn't a criminal." I quickly explained about DNA research and that it wasn't about seeking those with a criminal record.

Once that was explained he said, "Oh, okay, because I was going to say that your father wasn't a criminal. From what I can gather, he was just a very irresponsible man."

This, coupled with his comment about her "stepping out of line with the expectations of the times" gave me pause for thought. Did she "step out of line" or was she the victim of a crime?

I still didn't know.

I trusted Tom.

He was also loved and trusted by my mother, so much so that she told him about me before I reunited with her in 1993, even after she had rejected the offer to reunite in 1991.

He knew about me.

Knew my name was Melanie.

Were the other things he was told and shared with me truthful?

When had Tom ever lied to me?

What reason would he have to lie to me now?

Encouraging Me to Write

Tom doesn't read blogs and had no idea I shared my story on the blog.

I was on day number three of sharing the story on the blog, when he said, "Mel, you need to get this out there, you know. You need to write the story. I believe you have the ability to tell it in a way people will understand the good, the bad, what's happened to you, to her, to all of the girls and women back then."

I said, "Tom, it's interesting that you say that because I'm writing the story on the blog right now."

He was so excited and asked me to print out some things and send to him through the mail so he could read it.

He is proud of me.

"Don't stop, Deanna. Whatever you do, please don't stop," he said.

Another Call, Another Day

"You know, I have compassion for my wife and what she's been through," he says on another call. "At the same time I have such empathy for you. I know it's only right for you to have your father's name. It's just that the scars of the past affect her so much, she just won't go there because it brings up such terrible memories of the way she was treated by those who surrounded her."

"You don't have to explain," I said. "Right now it's not your place to be concerned about me. Your focus right now just needs to be her."

"I know," he said. "It is, and I'm there. But if I had those two words, I hope you know I'd give them to you in a second. I know how much you need them. But I don't have them. Oh, how I wish I did."

"I don't expect you to give me the two words, Tom. I would have never asked you. I certainly don't expect it now. Just take care of her."

Wiping my tears once more, I was amazed that he was even thinking of me or about my father's name.

But that's Tom.

Next Call—The Knot Tied Tight

"You know, you tied the knot tight, Mel. You made sure to tie it tight. Sixteen years for us now, remember that day? God, that was an amazing day."

We laugh.

"Yeah, of course I remember," I chuckled. "I try my best to tie the knots tight. A few have come loose, but yours has held well all these years, sixteen now."

"We've had a good run, her and me," he said as his voice broke.

"I can only hope we might have more years."

"I know."

Tears. Many tears.

We have these talks...

Talks about Judy's condition.

About what the world was like when I was born.

Africa.

The kids.

Food.

Writing.

Travel.

History.

Life.

Death.

Family.

The latest unique gift he found was a vegetable named "Larry" for Larry.

It had been in his car for a few months, he just kept forgetting to mail it.

Everything.

And nothing at all.

We usually don't have a call under two hours.

Reaching Out

Within twenty-four hours of Tom's first call, after a session with Melissa, I let him know I would reach out and make a call to Judy. I was afraid, but I had made a decision and was ready.

I would throw myself all in, come what may, and let Melissa clean up the mess later.

"Deanna, I don't want to hurt your feelings," he said, "but at this time it's not best."

He went on to explain that Judy's condition had sharply declined in the twenty-four hours after his initial call. After the magnitude of our falling out in February, he felt to talk to her would possibly have very negative effects on her current medical condition and her progress—even if we didn't discuss anything from the past. (Which I didn't plan on doing anyway.)

"I'm also worried about you," he said. "I don't want you to get hurt. And I'm afraid you might. She's not ready yet. It will be a bad thing for the both of you, and that's the last thing I want. I really understand where you both are coming from, Deanna."

More of the Unknown

I didn't know how long Judy had left.

Unless God or medical science or a combination of the two performed a miracle, I would be losing my mother for the fourth time.

It could be a few months.

A year.

More.

I wasn't sure.

There were roses and thorns, twists and turns yet to come, because it's just the way the story goes.

She was not at the point where it would be wise for us to have a call yet, per Tom's advice.

Some advised me saying, "Don't listen to Tom! Go to her and bust into her hospital room unannounced whether anybody wants you to or not."

That would have been foolish.

Tom was for me, not against me.

With every move she made, from ICU, to a hospital room, to a treatment facility, he gave me all the information. Address. Phone. Room. Updates on her condition. Nothing was hidden.

When he would give all the new contact information to me I would say, "Just to clarify, are you giving this to me because you want me to call or come? Do you think it's time to do that?"

"No," he would say, "I don't think it's best quite yet, but you know I'm just being open and giving you all the information. There should be no secrets. I want to keep you informed."

When she was stabilized enough for a call or visit, we would take it from there.

Tom wanted more than anything for this to happen.

It's just that he was trying to do it in such a way that it didn't worsen her condition.

"Deanna, in my mind, there's nothing more important in this than you having a mother and her having a daughter," he said.

Tears.

I wanted to believe that she wanted me.

Part of me was afraid to believe for that again. Just keepin' it real.

Tom said she wanted me.

He said he knew this his heart.

He said to believe that, no matter what February 28 kept screaming in my head.

Reality was:

She may not want to see me.

Or talk to me.

She never personally let me know she was sick or going in for surgery.

I don't think she wanted me to know.

Some said, "Don't worry about that. Be brave. Do what you did in 1993. Go anyway."

I was brave enough to do it.

That wasn't the issue.

My values are important to me.

Doing what I say I'm going to do.

Keeping my word.

The night I reunited with Judy in 1993 I promised her I wouldn't pressure her or remain in contact with her if she didn't want it. I hope she hadn't changed her mind – but if she had I wasn't going to dishonor her request especially in what may have been her final days, harassing her, even if I wanted my own way.

One reason I had such peace about the decision to not go busting the doors down at the wrong time was because of the six-page letter. It was loving and kind, and everything I ever wanted to say to her. There was nothing left unsaid on my end.

I didn't regret writing the letter even though the outcome was painful—in retrospect, I needed the peace that the letter now gives me. It assured me that even if it was never the right time to call or come, she already has all the words that I've ever wanted to tell her.

This is what happens when God writes the story. He knew I would need the six-page letter even more than she might have.

Fallout from History

They were never the same, these girls.

Society's reaction stripped them of their self-worth.

Who or what would my mother possibly be, had shame not gotten its ugly claws into her life, branding her a modern day leper, forever embedding her personal scarlet letter there as a constant default setting?

I hate what happened to my mother, and to four million women like her.

Who Stole Redemption?

Among other things, I hate that it twisted "redemption" into a sick theology for millions of people that would become standard doctrine for decades, and for many still is.

Girls were sold the lie that giving up a baby brought redemption. That God would forgive you, if you only paid the consequences, by your unselfish act of giving up your child for someone who could not have one. In time, you would forget. You would move on.

There is still this false theology perpetuated by some that you can be redeemed by giving up a baby. It is the standard bill of goods that is sold to many young pregnant girls in an effort to keep up with the supply and demand for infant relinquishments.

I get this question:

Are you anti-adoption, Deanna?

No.

I am pro-family.

I'm pro-preservation whenever possible. (And I know sometimes it isn't.)

I'm pro-parenting.

I'm pro-helping.

I'm pro-mentoring.

I'm pro-reaching-out to pregnant girls and women and saying, "What do you need?"

I've written thousands of words on this subject. But if I had to sum it up in one sentence it would be this. When a young lady becomes pregnant, the first question we need to ask her is, "How can I help you?"

What about this don't many understand? It's about reaching out a helping hand.

~~I just realized that sounds like Dr. Seuss.~~

~~I will help them in their need.~~

~~I will help them without greed.~~

~~I will help them with their child.~~

~~I will help when bills are piled.~~

~~I will help if they're sixteen.~~

~~I will bring them some green beans.~~

Okay seriously, friends. It's about helping.

"Oh Deanna, my church doesn't have a program for that..."

It doesn't take a program.

Just help.

Do what you can do.

Everyone from Christians to atheists to agnostics to Buddhists to Universalists read this story when it first published on my blog. My inbox was so full after I shared it there, that I would have to stay up until the middle of the night at times answering mail. I was awestruck and humbled by this, and I count readers as precious friends.

Perhaps many of you who are reading this right now don't believe in Jesus.

For the ones who do, I want to speak directly to something.

So if you are not a believer I ask you to let me speak to the Christians for a moment with a mini-refresher course in redemption.

A Few Reminders about Jesus in Case Anyone Forgot

Jesus redeems anyone who asks Him to.

He wants everyone to come to Him, and accepts them just as they are.

They do not have to give up a baby to receive forgiveness, redemption, acceptance, or a new start.

Redemption is not based upon what we can do, it's based upon what Jesus has already done.

Redemption is not by our sacrifice, but by His.

Redemption isn't about us giving something, it's about us receiving something.

If I were to write a book about adoption I've thought of calling it: *Who Stole Redemption?* Subtitle: *Put it Back on the Cross, Please.*

Redemption is only about one thing: coming to Jesus.

It does require coming to Jesus, but it doesn't require giving up your kids.

I have read the Bible cover to cover. Several times.

I know what the unpardonable sin is.

It isn't being a single mom.

~~Or having a tattoo.~~

Okay, unbelievers—you can tune in again now.

They Are All Around Us

Many of the four million would never darken the doors of a church—too much shame attached.

My mother is one of those women. She has absolutely no desire to walk in a church building and in the past twenty years the only time she's probably done so is when she visited me or attended a wedding.

Yes, that absolutely breaks my heart. It kills me.

The church was not there for my mother when she was pregnant with me.

She thinks, "Why would I want to be there now?"

Yet, there are many of the women from that time period who do attend services and sit there every week with a gaping hole in their hearts, doubtful that anyone would accept them if they shared their secret.

I've Seen It Myself

Recently, I spoke at an event and told part of my life story. There were girls on the front row—teenagers who looked at me with eyes wide as saucers, unable to comprehend any of what I was saying. It's simply unthinkable in this day and time to be sent away to hide.

However there were a group of older women on the back row.

Flat sensible shoes.

Pants that have give and take.

Wool nubby sweaters.

Short grayish hair and wire framed glasses.

I noticed as I spoke, they got emotional.

Wiped many tears.

At the conclusion several discreetly hugged me and tearfully whispered in my ear, "Thank you, thank you honey, you just don't know."

Yes. Yes I do.

I recognize a part of my mother in you.

You are a girl who went away.

And it slayed you.

And it still slays you at times.

And the people in your church have no idea.

And the thought of it still strikes fear in your heart to dare to speak it out loud.

Yes, I do know.

And I see you.

More than that, God sees you. He loves you with a love far beyond what you could ever comprehend.

The Call

Tom's call would come, sooner than I thought.

I would exit the car and head toward her door, legs like Jello with every step.

Because it had been this way throughout my life, I knew a power greater than my own would be with me, carrying me as I walked through the corridors of the hospital or wherever Tom summoned me.

It would take more courage this time than it ever did in 1993.

She was still worthy to be found.

Forthcoming

Restored,
Pursuing Wholeness When a Relationship is Broken,
the sequel to *Worthy To Be Found*
will be available in early 2015.

Sign up for Deanna's Adoptee Restoration enewsletter:
www.AdopteeRestoration.com
(enter your email in the right-hand column).
Receive notifications right away when this compelling
sequel to her story is available!

Acknowledgements

Entourage Publishing: You are THE BEST! *Worthy to Be Found* would still be on my blog, if not for you asking to publish it. I never imagined that it would be anywhere else but on the blog, but here we are. Thank you.

Laura Dennis: *Worthy to Be Found* wouldn't exist without you. You lovingly yet relentlessly pushed me to release it to the world in book format. You did it not just because you're my bestie, but because you believe in me—and are convinced the world needs to hear what I have to say on a broader scale. Our friendship is one of the greatest blessings I've ever received in my life. I cherish you.

Linda Boulanger at Tell Tale Book Covers: For putting up with my incessant tweaking to get it "just right." Thanks for going the extra mile and doing whatever it takes to make your clients happy. Those kinds of people are a rarity in this day and age, and you are one.

Gayle Lechner: My writing on the subject of adoption wouldn't have ever taken place were it not for you. Again and again in our private conversations you said, "PD, the world needs to hear this…" After lots of talks over crepes at IHOP, I finally listened to you and started the blog. My life immediately changed. The rest is history. For your incessant prodding, extraordinary editing skills, giving such insightful feedback and always loving and supporting me as you do, thank you.

Joanne Greer: For having my back for decades now since our days at The University of Valley Forge. Walking through the joys of life as well as the incredibly messy and painful parts and doing it with such grace. I love you so much, my bff and prayer partner.

Robin Davis: Thank you for the amazing gift of an additional edit on this project. You are the best and I so appreciate you!

Adoptee Restoration readers: I'm still amazed at your overwhelming response to my story. Without you, this book wouldn't exist because I never would have been convinced that my story was something anyone would have great interest in, until you showed me otherwise. I appreciate all of you more than words can say.

About the Author

Deanna Doss Shrodes is an Assemblies of God minister, serving for twenty-seven years in pastoral ministry. Currently she serves as the Director of Women's Ministries for the PenFlorida District of the Assemblies of God and is an in-demand speaker in the United States and abroad. In the adoption community, Deanna is best known for her blog, *Adoptee Restoration*. An award-winning writer, she is the author of *JUGGLE, Manage Your Time...Change Your Life!* She is a contributing author to five highly acclaimed anthologies, contributing author to *Chocolate for a Woman's Courage*, and a feature writer in scores of publications worldwide, including *The Huffington Post*. Deanna and her husband Larry make their home in the Tampa Bay area with their three children.

Made in the USA
Middletown, DE
19 May 2022

65959535R00136